PowerPoint 2007: Basic

Student Manual

PowerPoint 2007: Basic

VP and GM, Training Group:	Michael Springer
Series Product Managers:	Charles G. Blum and Adam A. Wilcox
Developmental Editor:	Kevin Ogburn
Copyeditor:	Cathy Albano
Keytester:	Bill Bateman
Series Designer:	Adam A. Wilcox
Cover Designer:	Abby Scholz

For more information contact:

Course Technology
25 Thomson Place
Boston, MA 02210

Or find us on the Web at: www.course.com

For permission to use material from this text or product, submit a request online at: www.thomsonrights.com

Any additional questions about permissions can be submitted by e-mail to: thomsonrights@thomson.com

Trademarks

Course ILT is a trademark of Course Technology.

Microsoft is a trademark or registered trademark of Microsoft Corporation in the United States and/or other countries.

Some of the product names and company names used in this book have been used for identification purposes only and may be trademarks or registered trademarks of their respective manufacturers and sellers.

Disclaimers

Course Technology reserves the right to revise this publication and make changes from time to time in its content without notice.

Course Technology is independent from Microsoft Corporation, and not affiliated with Microsoft in any manner. While this publication may be used in assisting individuals to prepare for a Microsoft Business Certification exam, Microsoft, its dedicated program administrator, and Course Technology do not warrant that use of this publication will ensure passing a Microsoft Business Certification exam.

1-4260-9766-2

Printed in the United States of America

1 2 3 4 5 WS 06 05 04 03

What is the Microsoft Business Certification Program?

The Microsoft Business Certification Program enables candidates to show that they have something exceptional to offer—proven expertise in Microsoft Office programs. The two certification tracks allow candidates to choose how they want to exhibit their skills, either through validating skills within a specific Microsoft product or taking their knowledge to the next level and combining Microsoft programs to show that they can apply multiple skill sets to complete more complex office tasks. Recognized by businesses and schools around the world, over 3 million certifications have been obtained in over 100 different countries. The Microsoft Business Certification Program is the only Microsoft-approved certification program of its kind.

What is the Microsoft Certified Application Specialist Certification?

The Microsoft Certified Application Specialist Certification exams focus on validating specific skill sets within each of the Microsoft® Office system programs. The candidate can choose which exam(s) they want to take according to which skills they want to validate. The available Application Specialist exams include:

- Using Microsoft® Windows Vista™
- Using Microsoft® Office Word 2007
- Using Microsoft® Office Excel® 2007
- Using Microsoft® Office PowerPoint® 2007
- Using Microsoft® Office Access 2007
- Using Microsoft® Office Outlook® 2007

What is the Microsoft Certified Application Professional Certification?

The Microsoft Certified Application Professional Certification exams focus on a candidate's ability to use the 2007 Microsoft® Office system to accomplish industry-agnostic functions, for example Budget Analysis and Forecasting, or Content Management and Collaboration. The available Application Professional exams currently include:

- Organizational Support
- Creating and Managing Presentations
- Content Management and Collaboration
- Budget Analysis and Forecasting

What do the Microsoft Business Certification Vendor of Approved Courseware logos represent?

Microsoft
C E R T I F I E D
Application
Specialist

Approved Courseware

Microsoft
C E R T I F I E D
Application
Professional

Approved Courseware

The logos validate that the courseware has been approved by the Microsoft® Business Certification Vendor program and that these courses cover objectives that will be included in the relevant exam. It also means that after utilizing this courseware, you may be prepared to pass the exams required to become a Microsoft Certified Application Specialist or Microsoft Certified Application Professional.

For more information

To learn more about the Microsoft Certified Application Specialist or Professional exams[1], visit www.microsoft.com/learning/msbc.

To learn about other Microsoft Certified Application Specialist approved courseware from Course Technology, visit www.courseilt.com.

---

[1]The availability of Microsoft Certified Application exams varies by Microsoft Office program, program version, and language. Visit www.microsoft.com/learning for exam availability.

Contents

Introduction

After reading this introduction, you will know how to:

A Use Course Technology ILT manuals in general.

B Use prerequisites, a target student description, course objectives, and a skills inventory to properly set your expectations for the course.

C Re-key this course after class.

Topic A: About the manual

Course Technology ILT philosophy

Course Technology ILT manuals facilitate your learning by providing structured interaction with the software itself. While we provide text to explain difficult concepts, the hands-on activities are the focus of our courses. By paying close attention as your instructor leads you through these activities, you will learn the skills and concepts effectively.

We believe strongly in the instructor-led class. During class, focus on your instructor. Our manuals are designed and written to facilitate your interaction with your instructor, and not to call attention to manuals themselves.

We believe in the basic approach of setting expectations, delivering instruction, and providing summary and review afterwards. For this reason, lessons begin with objectives and end with summaries. We also provide overall course objectives and a course summary to provide both an introduction to and closure on the entire course.

Manual components

The manuals contain these major components:

- Table of contents
- Introduction
- Units
- Course summary
- Quick reference
- Glossary
- Index

Each element is described below.

Table of contents

The table of contents acts as a learning roadmap.

Introduction

The introduction contains information about our training philosophy and our manual components, features, and conventions. It contains target student, prerequisite, objective, and setup information for the specific course.

Units

Units are the largest structural component of the course content. A unit begins with a title page that lists objectives for each major subdivision, or topic, within the unit. Within each topic, conceptual and explanatory information alternates with hands-on activities. Units conclude with a summary comprising one paragraph for each topic, and an independent practice activity that gives you an opportunity to practice the skills you've learned.

The conceptual information takes the form of text paragraphs, exhibits, lists, and tables. The activities are structured in two columns, one telling you what to do, the other providing explanations, descriptions, and graphics.

Course summary

This section provides a text summary of the entire course. It is useful for providing closure at the end of the course. The course summary also indicates the next course in this series, if there is one, and lists additional resources you might find useful as you continue to learn about the software.

Quick reference

The quick reference is an at-a-glance job aid summarizing some of the more common features of the software.

Glossary

The glossary provides definitions for all of the key terms used in this course.

Index

The index at the end of this manual makes it easy for you to find information about a particular software component, feature, or concept.

Manual conventions

We've tried to keep the number of elements and the types of formatting to a minimum in the manuals. This aids in clarity and makes the manuals more classically elegant looking. But there are some conventions and icons you should know about.

Item	Description
Italic text	In conceptual text, indicates a new term or feature.
Bold text	In unit summaries, indicates a key term or concept. In an independent practice activity, indicates an explicit item that you select, choose, or type.
`Code font`	Indicates code or syntax.
`Longer strings of ▶ code will look ▶ like this.`	In the hands-on activities, any code that's too long to fit on a single line is divided into segments by one or more continuation characters (▶). This code should be entered as a continuous string of text.
Select **bold item**	In the left column of hands-on activities, bold sans-serif text indicates an explicit item that you select, choose, or type.
Keycaps like ⏎ ENTER	Indicate a key on the keyboard you must press.

Hands-on activities

The hands-on activities are the most important parts of our manuals. They are divided into two primary columns. The "Here's how" column gives short instructions to you about what to do. The "Here's why" column provides explanations, graphics, and clarifications. Here's a sample:

Do it!

A-1:   Creating a commission formula

Here's how	Here's why
1 Open Sales	This is an oversimplified sales compensation worksheet. It shows sales totals, commissions, and incentives for five sales reps.
2 Observe the contents of cell F4	F4 ▼ = =E4*C_Rate
	The commission rate formulas use the name "C_Rate" instead of a value for the commission rate.

For these activities, we have provided a collection of data files designed to help you learn each skill in a real-world business context. As you work through the activities, you will modify and update these files. Of course, you might make a mistake and therefore want to re-key the activity starting from scratch. To make it easy to start over, you will rename each data file at the end of the first activity in which the file is modified. Our convention for renaming files is to add the word "My" to the beginning of the file name. In the above activity, for example, a file called "Sales" is being used for the first time. At the end of this activity, you would save the file as "My sales," thus leaving the "Sales" file unchanged. If you make a mistake, you can start over using the original "Sales" file.

In some activities, however, it might not be practical to rename the data file. If you want to retry one of these activities, ask your instructor for a fresh copy of the original data file.

Topic B: Setting your expectations

Properly setting your expectations is essential to your success. This topic will help you do that by providing:

- Prerequisites for this course
- A description of the target student
- A list of the objectives for the course
- A skills assessment for the course

Course prerequisites

Before taking this course, you should be familiar with personal computers and the use of a keyboard and a mouse. Furthermore, this course assumes that you've completed the *Windows XP: Basic* course or have equivalent experience.

Target student

The target student for the course is an individual who wants to learn the basic features of PowerPoint to create effective presentations by using the drawing tools, clip art, WordArt, charts, and tables. You need little or no experience using PowerPoint.

Microsoft Certified Application Specialist certification

This course is designed to help you pass the Microsoft Certified Application Specialist exam for PowerPoint 2007. For comprehensive certification training, you should complete both of the following courses:

- *PowerPoint 2007: Basic*
- *PowerPoint 2007: Advanced*

Course objectives

These overall course objectives will give you an idea about what to expect from the course. It is also possible that they will help you see that this course is not the right one for you. If you think you either lack the prerequisite knowledge or already know most of the subject matter to be covered, you should let your instructor know that you think you are misplaced in the class.

Note: In addition to the general objectives listed below, specific Microsoft Certified Application Specialist exam objectives are listed at the beginning of each topic (where applicable). To download a complete mapping of exam objectives to ILT Series content, go to: www.virtualrom.com/7DA99C5AA

After completing this course, you will know how to:

- Explore the PowerPoint environment; open and run a presentation; use Help options; and close a presentation and PowerPoint.

- Create a new presentation; add new slides to it; save and update changes; rearrange and delete slides; and insert slides from another presentation.

- Format text and bulleted lists; use the Find, Replace, Cut, Copy, and Paste commands; and align text.

- Draw objects by using tools in the Drawing group; format, modify, move, rotate, and delete drawn objects by using groups on the Drawing Tools Format tab; add text to drawn objects; and apply formatting to drawn objects.

- Use WordArt to create visually appealing text objects; add images to a slide and modify images by using the Picture Tools tab options; and add and modify clip art images.

- Add a table to a presentation, enter text in the table, and format the table; create and modify a chart by using the Create Chart dialog box and the options on the Chart Tools tabs; and create and modify an IGX chart by using the options on the IGX Graphic Tools tabs.

- Modify a presentation by using a template; make global changes to a presentation by using the Master Slide view; specify slide transitions and timings; add speaker notes and footers to a slide show; and set up a slide show for a speaker and for a kiosk.

- Proof a presentation for mistakes by using the Spell Check, AutoCorrect, and Thesaurus features; prepare a presentation to be shown by customizing and previewing it; and use the Print dialog box and the Print Preview tab to specify printing options for an entire presentation, an individual slide, handouts, and notes pages.

Skills inventory

Use the following form to gauge your skill level entering the class. For each skill listed, rate your familiarity from 1 to 5, with 5 being the most familiar. *This is not a test.* Rather, it is intended to provide you with an idea of where you're starting from at the beginning of class. If you're wholly unfamiliar with all the skills, you might not be ready for the class. If you think you already understand all of the skills, you might need to move on to the next course in the series. In either case, you should let your instructor know as soon as possible.

Skill	1	2	3	4	5
Opening, updating, and closing presentations					
Navigating a presentation					
Creating new presentations					
Adding, editing, rearranging, and deleting slides					
Adding, editing, and formatting slide text					
Inserting slides from other presentations					
Copying text formatting					
Changing bullet styles					
Finding and replacing text					
Copying and pasting slide text					
Drawing and formatting shapes					
Duplicating, deleting, and moving objects					
Resizing, rotating, and aligning objects					
Adding text to objects and drawing text boxes					
Adding and modifying WordArt					
Inserting and modifying a picture					
Arranging and grouping overlapping items					
Inserting and modifying clip art					
Adding, modifying, and formatting tables					
Creating and formatting charts and diagrams					
Creating presentations based on templates					
Applying design themes					

Skill	1	2	3	4	5
Modifying the slide master					
Creating new slide masters					
Specifying slide transitions and timings					
Adding and formatting speaker notes					
Setting up slide shows					
Proofing presentations					
Previewing and running presentations					
Printing presentations					

Topic C: Re-keying the course

If you have the proper hardware and software, you can re-key this course after class. This section explains what you'll need in order to do so, and how to do it.

Hardware requirements

Each student's personal computer should have:

- A keyboard and a mouse
- Pentium 500 MHz processor (or higher)
- 256 MB RAM (or higher)
- 2.5 GB of available hard drive space
- CD-ROM drive
- SVGA at 1024 × 768, or higher resolution monitor

Software requirements

You will need the following software:

- Windows XP, Windows Vista, or Windows Server 2003
- Microsoft PowerPoint 2007
- Microsoft Excel 2007
- A printer is required to complete Activity C-3 in the Proofing and delivering presentations unit, although students can opt not to print

Setup instructions to re-key the course

Before you re-key the course, you will need to perform the following steps.

1 Download the latest critical updates and service packs from www.windowsupdate.com.

2 From the Control Panel, open the Display Properties dialog box and apply the following settings:

- Theme — Windows XP
- Screen resolution — 1024 by 768 pixels
- Color quality — High (24 bit) or higher

If you choose not to apply these display settings, your screens might not match the screen shots in this manual.

3 If necessary, reset any PowerPoint 2007 defaults that you have changed. If you do not wish to reset the defaults, you can still re-key the course, but some activities might not work exactly as documented.

4 Create a folder named Student Data at the root of the hard drive. For a standard hard drive setup, this will be C:\Student Data.

5   Download the student data files for the course. (If you do not have an Internet connection, you can ask your instructor for a copy of the data files on a disk.)

    a   Connect to www.courseilt.com/instructor_tools.html.

    b   Click the link for Microsoft PowerPoint 2007 to display a page of course listings, and then click the link for PowerPoint 2007: Basic.

    c   Click the link for downloading the student data files, and follow the instructions that appear on your screen.

6   Copy the data files to the Student Data folder.

CertBlaster exam preparation software

If you plan to take the Microsoft Certified Application Specialist exam for PowerPoint 2007, we encourage you to use the CertBlaster pre- and post-assessment software that comes with this course. To download and install your free software:

1   Go to www.courseilt.com/certblaster.

2   Click the link for PowerPoint 2007.

3   Save the .EXE file to a folder on your hard drive. (Note: If you skip this step, the CertBlaster software will not install correctly.)

4   Click Start and choose Run.

5   Click Browse and then navigate to the folder that contains the .EXE file.

6   Select the .EXE file and click Open.

7   Click OK and follow the on-screen instructions. When prompted for the password, enter **c_603**.

Unit 1

Getting started

Unit time: 30 minutes

Complete this unit, and you'll know how to:

A Explore the PowerPoint environment.

B Get help by using PowerPoint's Help options.

Topic A: The PowerPoint window

Explanation

PowerPoint 2007 is part of the Microsoft Office suite. You can use PowerPoint to create presentations that can combine text, graphics, charts, clip art, and WordArt. These presentations can then be shown at to a single person or to a large audience.

If you're accustomed to previous versions of PowerPoint, you might initially be disoriented by the new interface. However, PowerPoint 2007 is designed to give you easy access to every command and feature of PowerPoint, and the new features will make creating visually appealing slide shows much easier.

Starting PowerPoint

To start PowerPoint, click the Start button and choose All Programs, Microsoft Office, Microsoft Office PowerPoint 2007. Every time you start PowerPoint, a new blank presentation appears in the application window and the Home tab is active by default.

The Office button

The File menu from previous versions of PowerPoint has been replaced by the Office button, located at the window's top-left, as shown in Exhibit 1-1. You can use the Office button to display a menu with commands for opening, saving, and performing other actions on files.

Office button

Exhibit 1-1: The Office button

Opening presentations

To open an existing presentation:

1   Click the Office button and choose Open. The Open dialog box appears.
2   From the Look in list, select the folder and file name of the presentation you want to open.
3   Click Open.

Running presentations

After a presentation is open, you can start adding text to the slide that appears in the PowerPoint window. When you're ready to display a presentation to your intended audience, you need to run a slide show. To run a slide show, activate the Slide Show tab at the top of the window to display the Slide Show controls. The area at the top of the window displaying the tabs and controls is called the *Ribbon*. On the Slide Show tab, click From Beginning to begin playing the slide show from the first slide.

Moving between slides

When you run a slide show, PowerPoint displays one slide at a time. You can advance the slides manually, or have PowerPoint advance the slides automatically. To move to the next slide in the show, you can:

- Click the mouse.
- Right-click and choose Next from the shortcut menu.
- Press the Page Down key.

To move to the previous slide, right-click and choose Previous, or press the Page Up key. To end the slide show at any time, press the Escape key.

A-1: Opening and running a presentation

Here's how	Here's why
1 Click **Start** and choose **All Programs**, **Microsoft Office**, **Microsoft Office PowerPoint 2007**	To start Microsoft PowerPoint. By default, a new, blank presentation opens.
Observe the screen	You'll see the PowerPoint window, which contains a blank presentation.
2 Click	(The Office button is in the upper-left corner of the program window.) To display a list of commonly used file commands.
Choose **Open**	To display the Open dialog box.
3 From the Look in list, navigate to the current unit folder	To view the contents of the current unit folder.
4 Select **Outlander Spices**	You'll open this presentation.
5 Click **Open**	To open the presentation. The first slide appears in the PowerPoint window.
6 Activate the Slide Show tab at the top of the window	To display the Slide Show controls.
In the Start Slide Show group, click **From Beginning**	To start the slide show from the first slide.
7 Observe the first slide	This is the title slide.
8 Click the left mouse button	To move to the next slide. You'll see a slide titled "Gourmet Collection."
9 Click the mouse again	To see a slide with formatted text and clip art.
10 Move to the next slide	(Click the mouse.) This is the fourth slide; it contains a table.
11 Move to the next slide	To see the fifth slide, which contains a chart.

12	Press `PAGE UP`	To move to the previous slide. You can use the Page Up and Page Down keys to view all the slides in the presentation.
13	Right-click the slide	To display the shortcut menu.
	Choose **Previous**	To move to the previous slide.
14	Click three times	To move three slides forward to see a slide containing a bar chart.
	Move to the last slide	To see a slide containing an organization chart.
	Click the left mouse button	To end the slide show. You'll see a black screen.
15	Click the mouse	To exit the show and return to the first slide.

The PowerPoint environment

Explanation

The PowerPoint window has several components that help you interact with the program. Exhibit 1-2 shows some of these components. If you're accustomed to previous versions of PowerPoint, you'll notice that the new version introduces significant changes to the interface.

Exhibit 1-2: The components of the PowerPoint 2007 window

The following table describes the components of the PowerPoint window.

Item	Description
Title bar	Displays the name of the current document.
Quick Access toolbar	Contains frequently used commands (by default, Save, Undo, and Repeat/Redo). Can be customized to include the commands you specify.
Ribbon	Contains PowerPoint's primary tools, commands, and other features, divided among tabs named Home, Insert, Design, Animations, Slide Show, Review, View, and Developer, as well as several contextual tabs. The items in each tab are organized into several groups.
Ribbon groups	Contain groupings of controls within a tab. Each tab contains several groups.
Slide	Displays the text and graphics that you type and edit. When you click a text placeholder, the flashing vertical line in the document area is called the *insertion point*, which indicates the location at which text will appear as you type.
Status bar	Contains the status information, View button, window switching buttons, and the document zoom slider.
Scrollbars	You can use the horizontal and vertical scrollbars to view parts of the presentation that don't currently fit in the window.

Gallery and list previews

In PowerPoint 2007, one way you can apply settings is by selecting an option from a gallery or list. The items in a gallery and in some lists are displayed as sample previews of how they will affect the current slide, rather than simply as a list of named options. For example, the Themes gallery on the Design tab in the Ribbon displays thumbnails of how each theme will look when applied to a slide.

In addition, some galleries and lists use *live preview*. When you move the pointer over options in a gallery or list that uses live preview, each option is previewed on the current slide. For example, moving the pointer over each font in the Font list causes any selected text on the current slide to appear in that font temporarily.

A-2: Examining the PowerPoint environment

Here's how	Here's why
1 Observe the title bar	Outlander Spices - Microsoft PowerPoint
	The title bar displays the current presentation's name (Outlander Spices) and the program name (Microsoft PowerPoint).
2 Observe the Ribbon	(Located at the top of the PowerPoint window under the title bar.) Most of PowerPoint's tools, commands, and other features are divided among the tabs on the Ribbon.
3 Activate the Home tab	To display the Home tab options.
4 Observe the groups on the Home tab	The Home tab includes the Clipboard, Slides, Font, Paragraph, Drawing, and Editing groups.
5 Activate the Insert tab	To display the Insert tab options.
In the Illustrations group, point to **Picture**, as shown	
	A ScreenTip appears, describing the functionality of the button.
6 Activate the Design tab	
In the Themes group, point to one of the theme icons	
	To see a live preview of the theme applied to the current slide.
Point away from the icons in the Themes group	The current slide returns to its original appearance.

7 In the Background group, click as shown

(The Dialog Box Launcher.) To open the Format Background dialog box. Some groups display a Dialog Box Launcher at the bottom-right corner, which opens a dialog box containing additional settings.

   Click **Close**

To close the dialog box.

8 Observe the slide

It has a title layout with text on it.

9 Point to the text on the slide

The pointer changes to an I-beam.

   Click the text

To place the insertion point in the text.

10 Observe the scrollbar

Use the vertical scrollbar to navigate among the slides while you're creating them.

11 Observe the status bar

(At the bottom of the PowerPoint window.) The left part of the status bar indicates which slide is selected and the total number of slides. The status bar also includes the name of the current theme, view buttons, and magnification controls.

Presentation views

Explanation

You can view a presentation in any one of three views: Normal, Slide Sorter, and Slide Show. You switch between these views by clicking the corresponding button.

View Name	Button	Description
Normal view		The default view, which you'll usually work in as you create slides. It contains two tabs on the left and a Slide pane on the right. The two tabs on the left are the Slides tab and the Outline tab.
Slide Sorter view		Provides a miniature view of all the slides in a presentation so you can view multiple slides at once. You can arrange the order of the slides by using this view.
Slide Show view		Provides a full-screen view of your presentation. Any special effects you add to your presentation, such as transitions and timings, are visible during the slide show.

Outline tab and Slides tab

In Normal view, there are two tabs to the left of the Slide pane: the Slides tab and the Outline tab. The Slides tab displays thumbnails of the slides. The Outline tab displays the slide text as an outline that you can use to organize and develop the content of the presentation. No matter which of these tabs you use, the Slide pane will still be visible.

Do it!   **A-3:   Observing views**

Here's how	Here's why
1 Click as shown	
	(In the left pane.) To display the Outline tab.
Observe the Outline tab	You'll see an outline of all the text in the presentation.
2 Activate the Slides tab	
3 Click ⊞	(The Slide Sorter button is on the status bar.) To switch to Slide Sorter view. All the slides now appear as thumbnails in the Slide pane. You can use this view to rearrange the order of the slides.
4 Click ⬚	(The Slide Show button is on the status bar.) To run the slide show from the current slide.
5 Press (ESC)	To end the slide show.
6 Click ▣	(The Normal button is on the status bar.) To switch to Normal view.

Adjusting magnification

Explanation

You can change the magnification of a slide in Normal view by changing the zoom level. To do so, use the zoom controls on the status bar, shown in Exhibit 1-3.

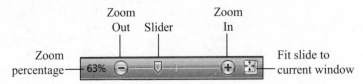

Exhibit 1-3: The zoom controls

Zoom in on a slide

To quickly increase the magnification level of the slide, click the Zoom In button, drag the slider to the right, or click the zoom percentage to open the Zoom dialog box. In the dialog box, set a higher zoom percentage and click OK.

Zoom out on a slide

To zoom out on a slide, click the Zoom Out button, drag the slider to the left, or click the zoom percentage to open the Zoom dialog box. Change the zoom to a lower percentage and click OK.

Do it!

A-4: Zooming in and out on a slide

Here's how	Here's why
1 Observe the zoom controls	On the right side of the status bar.
2 Point to the slider	You'll quickly zoom out.
Drag to the left	(Without releasing the mouse button.) To decrease the slide view, making it smaller.
Drag to the right	(Without releasing the mouse button.) To increase the slide view, making it bigger.
Release the mouse button	To change the slide view magnification.
3 Click the Zoom Out button twice	To decrease the zoom level by increments of 10%.
4 Click the Zoom In button twice	To increase the zoom level by increments of 10%.
5 Click the zoom percentage	To open the Zoom dialog box.
Observe the dialog box	
	Under Zoom to, you select a zoom level, or in the Percent box, you enter the desired zoom level.
Under Zoom to, select **33%**	To reduce the zoom level.
Click **OK**	To close the dialog box and view the slide at 33%.
6 Click ▨	(The Fit the slide to current window button.) To return the slide view to the default percentage.

Closing a presentation and PowerPoint

Explanation

You can close a PowerPoint presentation by clicking the Office button and choosing Close, or by pressing Ctrl+W.

There also are several ways to close the PowerPoint program:

- Click the Office button and at the bottom of the menu, click Exit PowerPoint.
- Click the Close button in the top-right corner of the title bar, shown in Exhibit 1-4. If multiple files are open, this button closes the active file. If one or no files are open, then this button closes the program.
- Press Alt+F4.

Close button

Exhibit 1-4: The Close button

Do it!

A-5: Closing a presentation and closing PowerPoint

Here's how	Here's why
1 Click ![Office button]	(The Office button.) To display the menu.
Choose **Close**	(If prompted to save your changes, click No.) To close the presentation.
2 Click ![Office button]	To display the menu.
Click **Exit PowerPoint**	(Located at the bottom of the menu.) To close PowerPoint.

Topic B: Getting help

Explanation

You can use the Help system to access program information and instructions as you work. To access Help, click the Microsoft Office PowerPoint Help icon at the top-right of the document window. (If you're connected to the Internet, you can access online Help information as well.)

In the PowerPoint Help window, shown in Exhibit 1-5, click the Home button to browse Help topics. Help works like a Web browser—each topic is a hyperlink that, when clicked, displays information about that topic. You also can display a table of contents by clicking the Show Table of Contents button. In addition, you can enter a word or phrase in the Search box to locate Help articles containing that word or phrase.

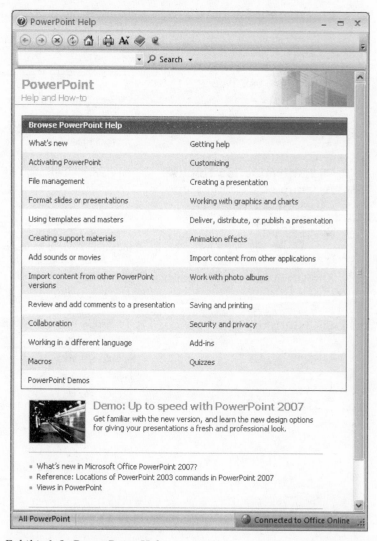

Exhibit 1-5: PowerPoint Help

Do it!

B-1: Using Microsoft Office PowerPoint Help

Here's how	Here's why
1 Start PowerPoint	(Click Start, and choose All Programs, Microsoft Office, Microsoft Office PowerPoint 2007.) A blank presentation opens.
2 At the top-right of the document window, click [?]	(The Microsoft Office PowerPoint Help icon.) To open PowerPoint Help.
3 Click **What's New**	To display a list of topics describing changes in PowerPoint 2007.
4 Click **Use the Ribbon**	To display an article describing the Ribbon.
5 Click [🏠]	To return to the initial Help content categories.
6 In the Search box, type **extensions**	extensions ▾ 🔍 Search
Click **Search**	To search for Help topics containing the term "extensions."
7 Click **Introduction to new file name extensions and Office XML Formats**	To display information about that topic.
8 Click [📖]	(The Show Table of Contents button.) To show the table of contents in a pane to the left.
9 Scroll up in the Table of Contents pane	If necessary.
10 Click **Getting Help**	To display the articles in that category.

Click any article	**Table of Contents**
	 📖 What's new
	 📖 Getting help
	     ? Reference: Locations of PowerPoint
	     ? Create a basic presentation in Powe
	     📄 Up to speed with PowerPoint 2007
	     ? Views in PowerPoint

11 Click [📘]	(The Hide Table of Contents button.) To hide the table of contents pane.
12 Close PowerPoint Help	Click the Close button.

Unit summary: Getting started

Topic A   In this topic, you opened a presentation and viewed it as a **slide show**. You also examined the PowerPoint environment, and switched among Normal, Slide Sorter, and Slide Show views. You also adjusted **magnification** in Normal view.

Topic B   In this topic, you used **PowerPoint Help** to locate information on various PowerPoint topics.

Independent practice activity

In this activity, you'll open a presentation and switch among views. You'll adjust the magnification, and you'll close the presentation.

1 Start PowerPoint, if necessary.

2 Open Training (from the current unit folder).

3 Switch to Slide Sorter view.

4 Switch to Slide Show view. View each slide, and then end the slide show.

5 In Normal view, change the Zoom percentage to 21%.

6 Close the presentation and PowerPoint (you don't need to save changes).

Review questions

1 One way to run a slide show is to activate the Slide Show tab, and then in the Start Slide Show group, click what button?

2 List the methods you can use to advance slides manually when running a slide show.

3 To end the slide show at any time, which key should you press?

4 Define the Quick Access toolbar.

5 What does the live preview feature do?

6 List the three views you can use to view a presentation.

Unit 2

New presentations

Unit time: 40 minutes

Complete this unit, and you'll know how to:

A Create a basic presentation by adding slides and inserting text on each slide.

B Save a presentation by using the Save and Save As commands.

C Rearrange and delete slides by using options in Normal view and Slide Sorter view.

D Insert slides by using slides from another presentation.

Topic A: Creating new presentations

This topic covers the following Microsoft Certified Application Specialist exam objectives for PowerPoint 2007.

#	Objective
1.1.1	Create presentations from blank presentations
1.1.3	Create presentations from existing presentations
1.5	Arrange slides
	• Insert or delete slides

New presentation options

Explanation

To create a new presentation in PowerPoint 2007, click the Office button and choose New to open the New Presentation dialog box, shown in Exhibit 2-1. Under Templates, there are several options available. Select an option to indicate the type of new document you want to create.

New presentations from existing presentations

You might want to create a new presentation that includes much of the same content from an existing presentation. You could create the new presentation based on the existing presentation, and you could then modify the new presentation as necessary.

To create a new presentation based on an existing presentation:

1　Click the Office button and choose New to open the New Presentation dialog box.
2　Under Templates, select New from existing to open the New from Existing Presentation dialog box.
3　Select the existing presentation and click Create New. The new presentation is identical to the presentation on which it was based. You can save it with a new name.
4　Save the new presentation.

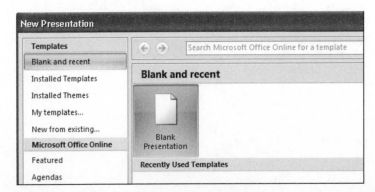

Exhibit 2-1: The New Presentation dialog box.

Do it!

A-1:   Creating a presentation from an existing presentation

Here's how	Here's why
1 Start Microsoft Office PowerPoint 2007	(Click Start and choose All Programs, Microsoft Office, Microsoft Office PowerPoint 2007). A new, blank presentation opens.
Close the blank presentation	Click the Office button and choose Close.
2 Click the Office button and choose **New**	To open the New Presentation dialog box.
3 Under Templates, click **New from existing**	To open the New from Existing Presentation dialog box.
Select **Training**	In the current unit folder.
Click **Create New**	To create a new presentation based on the Training presentation. You'll now save and name the new presentation.
4 Click 🖫	(The Save button is on the Quick Access toolbar.) To open the Save As dialog box.
5 In the File name box, edit the text to read **My training**	
Navigate to the current unit folder and click **Save**	The new presentation is identical to the Training presentation. You could now customize the My training presentation.
6 Close the My training presentation	Click the Office button and choose Close.

New blank presentations

If you want to create a new presentation that starts out without any content, then you should create a new blank presentation. To create a new blank presentation:

1   Click the Office button and choose New to open the New Presentation dialog box.

2   Under Templates, select Blank and recent, if necessary.

3   Under Blank and recent, click Blank Presentation, if necessary.

4   Click Create.

Slide layouts

A new blank presentation contains one slide by default. That slide uses the Title Slide layout, but you can select a different layout for your slides from the Layout gallery, which is available in the Home tab's Slides group. There are nine default layouts to choose from, as shown in Exhibit 2-2. The default layouts are described in the following table.

Layout	Description
Title Slide	Includes a title and subtitle placeholder.
Title and Content	Includes a title placeholder and one content placeholder. This is the default slide layout. You can type text in the content placeholder, or click one of the icons at its center to specify other types of content, such as tables, charts, or pictures.
Section Header	Includes a text placeholder above a title placeholder.
Two Content	Includes a title placeholder and two content placeholders.
Comparison	Includes a title placeholder, and two content placeholders with text placeholder for adding labels.
Title Only	Includes only a slide title placeholder.
Blank	Doesn't include any placeholders.
Content with Caption	Includes a content placeholder along with two text placeholders for adding text to accompany the slide content.
Picture with Caption	Includes a picture placeholder along with two text placeholders for adding text to accompany the picture.

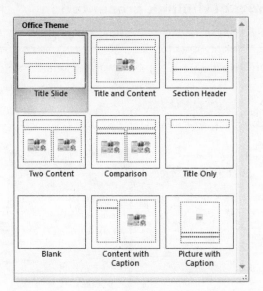

Exhibit 2-2: The nine layout options in the Layout gallery

A-2: Creating a new blank presentation

Here's how	Here's why
1 Click the Office button and choose **New**	To open the New Presentation dialog box.
2 Under Templates, verify that Blank and recent is selected	
3 Under Blank and recent, verify that Blank Presentation is selected	

New Presentation

Templates
- Blank and recent
- Installed Templates
- Installed Themes
- My templates...
- New from existing...

Microsoft Office Online
- Featured

Search Microso

Blank and recent

Blank Presentation

Recently Used Templates

Click **Create**	To create a new presentation that contains a single slide by default.
4 In the Home group, point to **Layout**	

Home   Insert   Desig

Layout
Reset

	When you click this button, a gallery is displayed that contains nine different slide layouts.
Click once	To display a list of the available slide layouts, as shown in Exhibit 2-2.
5 Observe the first layout	The first layout's name is "Title Slide." This is the layout that is automatically applied to the first slide in each presentation.
Observe the name for each layout	In the gallery.
Click **Layout** again	To close the gallery.

Entering text in slides

Explanation

After you select a slide layout, you can enter text on the slide. The Title Slide layout contains two placeholders for text: one placeholder for the title, and one for the subtitle. To enter text, click the placeholder text and begin typing.

Do it!

A-3:   Entering text in a slide

Here's how	Here's why
1 Point to the text in the title placeholder, as shown	Click to add title Click to add subtitle The pointer's shape changes when you point to the placeholder text.
Click the title placeholder text	(Click the text "Click to add title.") To place the insertion point in the title placeholder.
2 Type **Outlander Spices**	This will be the slide's title.
3 Click the subtitle placeholder text	(Below the title placeholder.) To display the insertion point.
Type **New Product Line**	
4 Click the slide anywhere outside the placeholder	To deselect it.

Adding and editing slides

After creating a new, blank presentation that has only one slide, you'll want to add more slides. To add a slide to a presentation, activate the Home tab on the Ribbon, and click the New Slide button in the Slides group to add a slide with the default layout, which is the Title and Content layout. To add a new slide with a different layout, click the New Slide button down arrow to display a gallery, and click the desired layout to add a new slide with that layout applied.

Adding bulleted text to a slide

The most commonly used slide layout is the Title and Content slide layout. It has two placeholders: one for the title and a second for the content. You can use this slide layout to add several types of content, but one of the most typical uses is to add bulleted text.

To insert bulleted text in the content placeholder:

1   Click the text in the content placeholder.
2   Type the text for the first bullet.
3   Press Enter to display a second bullet.
4   Type the text for the second bullet, and press Enter.
5   Continue this process to add text for additional bullets.
6   After adding bulleted items, click outside the placeholder to deselect it.

Modifying slide layout

You can modify a slide's layout by changing its placeholders. You can format, reposition, and resize a placeholder. You can also remove a placeholder from a slide by deleting it.

Deleting text and placeholders

To delete some of the text in a placeholder, select the text you want to remove, and press Delete or Backspace. To delete all the text in a placeholder, select the placeholder itself and press Delete. To select the placeholder, rather than the text within it, point to the edge of the placeholder and click. A four-headed arrow appears at the tip of the pointer when you're pointing to the correct location to select the placeholder itself.

After deleting the text you've added to a placeholder, you might want to delete the placeholder itself. When a placeholder displays its default placeholder text, you can select the placeholder and press Delete or Backspace to remove the placeholder from the slide.

Modifying placeholders

You can reposition a placeholder by dragging it. Point to any edge of a placeholder so that a four-headed arrow appears; then drag the placeholder to the new position.

In addition, you can modify a placeholder by changing its size. To resize a placeholder:

1   Click the edge of the placeholder so that sizing handles appear at each corner and along each edge.
2   Point to any of the sizing handles so that it becomes a two-headed arrow.
3   Drag the sizing handle to resize the placeholder.

Do it!   **A-4:   Adding and editing slides**

Here's how	Here's why
1 Click the top portion of the New Slide button	
	(In the Slides group.) To add a new slide to the presentation.
Observe the new slide	
	By default, it has the Title and Content slide layout applied to it. It has two placeholders: one for the slide's title and another for the content.
Observe the Slides tab on the left	It shows that the presentation has two slides.
2 Click the title placeholder text	(On the new slide.) To place the insertion point.
Type **Global Product Rollout**	To specify the slide's title.
3 Click the bulleted text placeholder	(Click the text in the content placeholder; don't click the icons at the center.) To place the insertion point in the placeholder. You are ready to enter text for the first bullet item.
4 Type **Starts in North America next month**	To create the first bullet item. The icons for adding other types of content disappear, because by typing, you've specified that this placeholder will contain text.
Press (↵ ENTER)	To add a second bullet.
5 Type **Financial plan**	To specify text for the second bullet.
Observe the slide	It contains a title and a bulleted list with two items.
6 Double-click **Financial**	To select the word.
Press (DELETE)	To remove the word from the slide.

7 Press (CTRL) + (Z)	To undo the last step. The word "Financial" is restored.
8 Point as shown	
	(On the placeholder box edge, but not on a sizing handle.) A four-headed arrow appears at the tip of the mouse pointer.
Click the mouse button	To select the placeholder box.
9 Press (DELETE)	To remove all the text from the placeholder. The placeholder is still on the slide but is empty, and it again displays the content icons.
10 Select the placeholder box again	Point to an edge of the placeholder so that the pointer appears with the four-headed arrow, and click.
Press (DELETE)	To remove the placeholder from the slide.
11 Press (CTRL) + (Z) twice	To undo the last two steps: deleting the placeholder and deleting the text from the placeholder.
12 Select the placeholder	
Point to the bottom-left sizing handle, as shown	
	You'll decrease the height and width of the placeholder. You can use the sizing handles on any of the corners to increase or decrease the height and width of the placeholder simultaneously.

13 Drag up and to the right

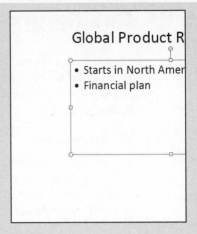

To decrease both the height and the width of the placeholder.

14 Point to the left center sizing handle, as shown

You'll decrease only the width of the placeholder.

Drag to the right

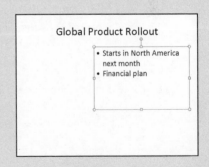

To decrease the width without changing the height.

15 Press ⌈CTRL⌉ + ⌈Z⌉ twice

To return the placeholder to its original size. You might need to press Ctrl+Z more than twice if you performed more than two resizing steps.

Topic B: Saving presentations

Explanation

As you create presentations, it's important to save your work frequently. By saving your work, you ensure that any text, graphics, or other elements in your presentation are written to your computer's hard disk and stored for future use. You save a presentation by using the Save and Save As commands.

The Save command

To save a presentation for the first time, you can start by either using the Save button on the Quick Access toolbar or clicking the Office button and choosing Save to open the Save As dialog box. Next, navigate to the desired location, edit the File name box to give your presentation a name, and then click Save.

Do it!

B-1: Saving a presentation in an existing folder

Here's how	Here's why
1 Click the Office button and choose **Save**	(Or click the Save button on the Quick Access toolbar.) To open the Save As dialog box.
2 Navigate to the current unit folder	(By using the Save in list.) You'll save your presentation in an existing folder.
3 Edit the File name box to read **New product line**	This will be the new presentation name.
Observe the Save as type box	By default, PowerPoint shows the type as PowerPoint Presentation.
Click **Save**	To save the presentation.
Observe the title bar	New product line - Microsoft PowerPoint
	You'll see that the file name appears in the title bar.

Updating presentations

Explanation

You have to specify a name and storage location for a presentation only when you save it for the first time. Each subsequent time you save a presentation, PowerPoint updates the file with your latest changes. To update the presentation, you can do any of the following:

- Click the Office button and choose Save.
- Click the Save button on the Quick Access toolbar.
- Press Ctrl+S.

Do it!

B-2:   Updating a presentation

Here's how	Here's why
1 Place the insertion point at the end of the second bullet item	You'll add more bullet items to the slide.
2 Press (↵ ENTER)	To add a third bullet to the slide.
3 Type **Discussion**	
Press (↵ ENTER)	
4 Type **Outstanding issues**	
Click outside the content placeholder	To deselect it.
5 Click ⊟	(The Save button is located on the Quick Access toolbar.) To save the changes made to the presentation.

The Save As command

After you've saved a presentation, you can save another copy of it with a different name or in a different location. To save a copy of a presentation, use the Save As command.

Saving presentations in new folders

To save a presentation in a new folder:

1 Click the Office button and choose Save As to open the Save As dialog box.
2 From the Save in list, select the appropriate location.
3 Click the Create New Folder button to open the New Folder dialog box.
4 In the Name box, specify a folder name. Click OK.
5 Verify that the Save in list displays the name of the new folder.
6 In the File name box, type a name for this copy of the presentation.
7 Click Save.

Compatibility with older versions of PowerPoint

PowerPoint 2007 presentations are saved with the extension ".pptx." Previous versions of PowerPoint have used the ".ppt" extension. Therefore, in order for older versions of PowerPoint to be able to open and read files created in PowerPoint 2007, you have to save them using the ".ppt" extension. To do so, click the Office button to display the menu. Point to Save As to display the Save a copy of the document options, as shown in Exhibit 2-3. Choose PowerPoint 97-2003 Presentation to save the document with a ".ppt" extension.

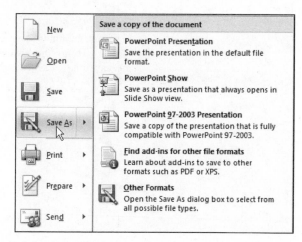

Exhibit 2-3: The Save a copy of the document options

If you are consistently saving presentations in the old ".ppt" format, then you can change PowerPoint's settings so that this is the default. To do so:

1 Click the Office button and click PowerPoint Options.
2 In the left pane, click Save.
3 From the Save files in this format list, select PowerPoint Presentation 97-2003.
4 Click OK.

XML

Beginning with this version of Office, all PowerPoint presentations use the Open XML format. This format makes it easier to use external data sources in PowerPoint files, makes the content of presentations easier to access using other applications, reduces file sizes, and improves data recovery. As explained previously, you still can save your presentations in the previous format, though, to make them compatible with older versions of PowerPoint. In addition, updates to older versions of PowerPoint will enable those versions to use the new XML format. Finally, Microsoft will make available converters to use with previous versions of PowerPoint.

Do it!

B-3: Saving a presentation in a new folder

Here's how	Here's why
1 Click the Office button	To display the menu.
Point to **Save As**	To display the "Save a copy of the document" options. You would use one of these options to save the file in a format that can be opened by older versions of PowerPoint, or as a PDF or XPS file.
Choose **Save As**	(Click Save As.) To open the Save As dialog box.
2 Navigate to the current unit folder	(If necessary.) You'll create a folder within the current unit folder to save your presentation.
3 Click	(The Create New Folder button is in the Save As dialog box.) To open the New Folder dialog box.
4 In the Name box, enter **My folder**	
Click **OK**	Notice that in the Save in list, "My folder" appears.
5 Edit the File name box to read **My first presentation**	
6 Display the Save As type list	Click the down arrow to the right of the list.
Observe the list	(Scroll through and read each line.) The list contains all the formats you can use to save your presentation.
Click the down arrow	To close the list.
Verify that **PowerPoint Presentation** is selected	This is the default file format.
7 Click **Save**	To save the presentation in the folder My folder.
Close the presentation	Click the Office button and choose Close.

Topic C: Rearranging and deleting slides

This topic covers the following Microsoft Certified Application Specialist exam objective for PowerPoint 2007.

#	Objective
1.5	Arrange slides
	• Insert or delete slides
	• Use the slide sorter to organize slides
	• Arrange slides by cutting, pasting, and dragging in normal view

Rearranging slides

Explanation

After you've added slides and text to your presentation, you might need to rearrange the order of slides or remove a slide. You can rearrange slides and remove slides in both Normal view and in Slide Sorter view. However, it is typically easier to rearrange slides in Slide Sorter view.

Moving slides in Normal view

In Normal view, you can use the Slides tab on the left side of the window to rearrange slides by dragging a slide thumbnail. As you drag, the insertion point shows you where the slide will appear after you release the mouse button. You can also move slides in Normal view by cutting or copying a slide and pasting it.

To cut or copy a slide and paste it in Normal view:

1 On the Slides tab, click a slide icon to select it.
2 On the Home tab, click the Cut or Copy button.
3 On the Slides tab, click above or below a slide icon to indicate the location where you want to paste the slide.
4 On the Home tab, click the Paste button.

Do it!

C-1: Rearranging slides in the Normal view

Here's how	Here's why
1 Open Gourmet Collections product line	From the current unit folder.
Save the presentation as **My Gourmet Collections product line**	
2 Observe the slide thumbnails	In the Slides tab on the left side of the window.
Scroll down	(In the Slides tab.) To view the last slide thumbnail.
Click the last slide thumbnail	You'll move slide 7 to a new location.
3 Drag the slide thumbnail as shown	
	As you drag the slide up, the Slide tab will scroll up as well.
Observe the pointer and the line	The pointer changes and has a gray box added to its shape. When you drag the mouse, a line appears to mark the slide's new position.
Release the mouse	To place the slide in the new position.
4 Observe the slides	The slide numbers are rearranged automatically. Slide 7 has become slide 5.
5 Update the presentation	

Using Slide Sorter view

Explanation

In Slide Sorter view, you can see many presentation slides at the same time, as shown in Exhibit 2-4. You can add, delete, and move slides in this view. You switch to Slide Sorter view by clicking the Slide Sorter button in the status bar.

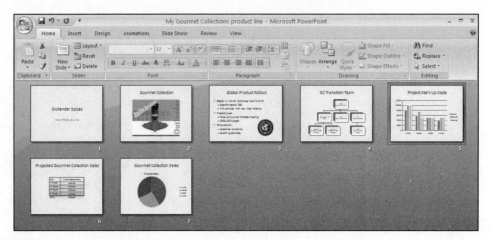

Exhibit 2-4: Slide Sorter view

Rearranging slides in Slide Sorter view

Because you can view many slides in Slide Sorter view, this is the easiest place to rearrange them in any order you want. You move a slide by dragging it to a new location in the presentation.

Do it! **C-2: Rearranging slides in Slide Sorter view**

Here's how	Here's why
1 Click ⊞	(In the status bar at the bottom of the window.) To switch to Slide Sorter view.
Observe the screen	You'll see thumbnail versions of all the slides in your presentation.
2 Observe the border around slide 5	You were working on this slide when you switched to Slide Sorter view. A border appears around the active slide, as shown in Exhibit 2-4.
3 Select the seventh slide	You'll move this slide.
Drag the slide before the fourth slide	
	A vertical line indicates where it will appear.
Release the mouse	To place the slide in its new position. Slide 7 has become slide 4.
4 Observe the slides	The slides have been rearranged, and the slide numbers reflect the new order.
5 Update the presentation	Click the Save button on the Quick Access toolbar.

Deleting slides in Normal view and Slide Sorter view

Explanation

You can remove slides from a presentation when you no longer need them. You can delete slides from Normal view or from Slide Sorter view. No matter which view you use to delete a slide, it is removed from the presentation and will no longer appear in any view. To delete slides from Normal view:

1   View the slide you want to remove.

2   On the Home tab, in the Slides group, click Delete.

You can use two techniques to delete slides from Slide Sorter view. Select the thumbnail for the slide you want to delete; then do either of the following:

- On the Home tab, in the Slides group, click Delete.
- Press Delete on the keyboard.

Do it!

C-3:   Deleting a slide in Slide Sorter view

Here's how	Here's why
1 Select the seventh slide	You'll delete this slide because it's no longer needed.
2 Press (DELETE)	(Or click Delete in the Slides group.) To delete the slide.
Observe the presentation	There are only six slides now.
3 Delete the fourth and fifth slides	
4 Switch to Normal view	(Click the Normal button in the status bar.) The presentation now contains only four slides.
5 Update the presentation	
Close the presentation	

Topic D: Using slides from other presentations

This topic covers the following Microsoft Certified Application Specialist exam objective for PowerPoint 2007.

#	Objective
2.3.1	Reuse slides from an existing presentation
	• Apply current slide masters to content

Copying slides between presentations

Explanation

You can copy slides from one presentation to another presentation. When you insert a slide from one presentation to another, the default setting causes the inserted slide to adopt the color and design theme of the presentation you insert it into. You can insert slides individually, or you can insert multiple slides simultaneously. To insert a slide from another presentation:

1 In the Slides group, click the down arrow on the New Slide button to display the drop-down gallery.

2 At the bottom of the gallery, click Reuse Slides to display the Reuse Slides task pane on the right side of the application window.

3 In the Reuse Slides pane, click the Browse down arrow, and choose Browse File to open the Browse dialog box.

4 In the Browse dialog box, select the desired presentation and click Open. Each slide in the selected presentation is displayed in the Reuse Slides pane.

5 At the bottom of the Reuse Slides pane, verify that Keep source formatting is cleared, if you want to apply the current presentation's slide masters to any inserted slides. Check the check box if you want the inserted slides to retain their slide masters.

6 In the Reuse Slides pane, click a slide to add it to the current presentation.

Changing the slide layouts

If you want to use a different layout for a slide, you can apply another layout style. To do so, select the slide and activate the Home tab. In the Slides group, click the Layout down arrow to display the Layout gallery. Click the desired layout to apply it.

D-1: Inserting slides from another presentation

Here's how	Here's why
1 Create a new, blank presentation	Click the Office button and choose New. In the New Presentation dialog box, click Blank Presentation and click Create.
2 Click the title placeholder	To select it so you can enter a title.
Type **Sales Update**	As the title for the slide.
3 In the subtitle placeholder, type **Corporate Plans**	Click the subtitle placeholder text, and type to add the subtitle.
4 Click the down arrow on the **New Slide** button	(In the Slides group.) To display the drop-down gallery.
At the bottom of the gallery, choose **Reuse Slides...**	To display the Reuse Slide pane on the right side of the application window.
5 In the Reuse Slides pane, click **Browse** as shown	
	You'll locate the presentation from which you'll insert slides.
Choose **Browse File...**	To open the Browse dialog box.
6 Navigate to the current unit folder	(In the Browse dialog box.) To view a list of presentations in the current unit folder.
Select **Gourmet Collections product line**	
Click **Open**	To view the slides in the selected presentation. They are added to the Reuse Slides pane.
7 Verify that Keep source formatting is cleared	(At the bottom of the Reuse Slides pane.) To ensure that the slides you insert will take on the background and text formats of the current presentation, as specified by the slide master.
8 Point to each slide in the Reuse Slides pane	(Point to each slide thumbnail, not the text next to it.) Notice that when you do, the slide is enlarged.
9 Click slide 3	(In the Reuse Slide pane.) To insert the "Global Product Rollout" slide as slide 2.
Click slide 5	To insert the "Projected Gourmet Collection Sales" slide as slide 3.

10	Observe the presentation	The two slides are now part of the new presentation. Notice that the content is the same, but the formatting is different, because the inserted slides now use the formatting from the current presentation's slide master.
11	On the Reuse Slides pane, click the Close button	
		To close the pane.
12	Save the presentation as **My sales update**	In the current unit folder.
	Close the presentation	

Unit summary: New presentations

Topic A   In this topic, you **created a new presentation** from a blank presentation. You also **added slides** to the presentation, **entered text** in a slide, and **edited the text**.

Topic B   In this topic, you used the Save As dialog box **to save a presentation**. Next, you **updated a presentation** by using the Save command. Then, you used the Save As dialog box to **save a presentation in a new location**.

Topic C   In this topic, you **moved slides** in both Normal view and Slide Sorter view. Then, you **deleted slides** in Slide Sorter view.

Topic D   In this topic, you **inserted slides from another presentation** into your presentation.

Independent practice activity

In this activity, you'll create a new presentation and you'll create new slides and add slide text. You'll also rearrange slides, and you'll save the presentation.

1 Create a new, blank presentation.

2 In the title slide, enter **My Company** as the title.

3 Use the Title and Content slide layout to add a new slide; add **New Locations In Major US Cities** as the title. Add **New York**, **Los Angeles**, and **Dallas** as a bulleted list.

4 Save the presentation as **My practice presentation** in the current unit folder.

5 Add another Title and Content slide, and add **Current Locations in Major US Cities** as the title. Add **Chicago**, **Miami**, and **Las Vegas** as a bulleted list.

6 Update the presentation.

7 Switch to Slide Sorter view.

8 Move slide 3 before slide 2.

9 Update and close the presentation.

Review questions

1 Name the nine slide layouts available in the Layout gallery.

2 List the steps you would perform to enter text on a title slide.

3 To add a slide to a presentation, activate the Home tab and click the _____ button in the Slides group to add a slide with the default layout.

4 How do you add a new slide with a layout other than the default layout?

5 How would you insert bulleted text in the content placeholder of a Title and Content slide?

6 To delete some of the text in a placeholder, select the text you want to remove, and then _____.

7 To save a copy of a presentation, use the _____ command.

8 What views can you use to rearrange the order of slides?

9 To delete a slide from Slide Sorter view, select the thumbnail for the slide you want to delete, and then _____ or _____.

10 When inserting slides from another presentation, what task pane do you use?

11 How can you apply a different layout to an existing slide?

Unit 3

Formatting slides

Unit time: 45 minutes

Complete this unit, and you'll know how to:

A Apply formatting to text and bulleted lists by using options on the Mini toolbar and in the Font and Paragraph groups.

B Modify text by using the Find, Replace, Cut, Copy, and Paste commands.

C Change the alignment of text by using options on the Mini toolbar and in the Font and Paragraph groups.

Topic A: Text formatting

This topic covers the following Microsoft Certified Application Specialist exam objectives for PowerPoint 2007.

#	Objective
2.2.3	Format font attributes
	• Change text size
	• Change text font
	• Change text color
	• Apply text such as bold, italic, underline, and shadow
2.2.4	Use the Format Painter to format text
2.2.5	Create and format bulleted and numbered lists
	• Add numbered lists
	• Format bullets
	• Format numbered lists
	• Promote and demote bullets and numbering

Slide text formatting

Explanation

After you add text to a slide, you can select the text and apply formatting to it. There are two types of formatting you can apply: character formatting and paragraph formatting.

Character and paragraph formatting

Character formatting is any formatting that you can apply to individual characters, and includes changing the font, font size, and type style (bold, italic, and underlining). *Paragraph formatting* is any formatting that can apply only to whole paragraphs, and includes text alignment, line spacing, bulleted lists, numbered lists, and so on.

The best way to understand the difference between the two types of formatting is to focus on what happens to the selected text. For example, when you select a specific section of text and apply character formatting, the formatting is applied only to the selected text. On the other hand, when applying paragraph formatting, you can select an entire paragraph(s), part of the paragraph(s), or just place the insertion point in a paragraph and apply the paragraph formatting. When you do, any paragraph that is partly or fully selected or even has the insertion point in it will have the formatting applied to all of it.

Font group and Mini toolbar

After the text is selected, there are two main ways to apply character formatting. You can use the button and options in the Font group on the Home tab, or use the Mini toolbar.

Font group

With the redesign of Office 2007, almost all of the commonly used features are now stored in easy-to-access groups organized on the tabs. The Font group includes the Font and Font Size lists, as well as buttons and the Dialog Box Launcher in the bottom-right corner, shown in Exhibit 3-1. The buttons include Bold, Italic, Underline, and Shadow, among others.

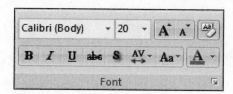

Exhibit 3-1: The Font group

Mini toolbar

The *Mini toolbar* is a floating palette that appears immediately after you select text on a slide. The Mini toolbar contains some of the formatting options available in the Font and Paragraph groups. After you select some text, the Mini toolbar appears but is almost transparent until you activate it by pointing to it. When you do, you have access to the most commonly used features based on your selection. Exhibit 3-2 shows the features available on the Mini toolbar when text on a slide is selected.

Exhibit 3-2: The Mini toolbar

The Mini toolbar will go away if you move the pointer too far away from it after making the selection. You can display the Mini toolbar at any time by right-clicking the selected text.

Selecting text

You can use several techniques to select text on PowerPoint slides. The following table describes these techniques.

Technique	Description
Drag across text	Point next to the first word you want to select, and drag across one or more words to select them.
Double-click word	Point to a word and click two times quickly without moving the pointer to select the word.
Triple-click word	Point to a word and click three times quickly without moving the pointer to select the entire paragraph.
Press Ctrl+A	Click within a text placeholder to place the insertion point; then press Ctrl+A to select all the text within the placeholder.
Shift-click	Place the insertion point where you want to begin the selection; then point to where you want to end the selection, press Shift, and click. The text between the two locations is selected.

Do it!　　**A-1:　Applying bold and italic formatting**

Here's how	Here's why
1　Open Project phase one	(From the current unit folder.) You'll format the text in this presentation.
2　Save the presentation as **My project phase one**	
3　Double-click **Outlander**	(In the title placeholder.) To select the word "Outlander." You'll format the title of the first slide.
4　Click [**B**]	(The Bold button is in the Font group.) To apply bold formatting to the selected word.
5　Select **Spices**	Double-click the word, but don't move the mouse pointer.
Observe the slide	Notice that there is a floating toolbar that is almost completely transparent right near the selection.
Point to the Mini toolbar	To activate it.
Click the **Bold** button, as shown	
	(The Bold button on the Mini toolbar.) To apply bold formatting to the selection.
6　Triple-click **Project**	(In the subtitle placeholder.) To select all three words in the subtitle. You'll italicize this text.
Activate the Mini toolbar	(Point to it.) If you can't see the Mini toolbar, select the text again and point to the Mini toolbar.
Click the **Italic** button, as shown	
	(The Italic button on the Mini toolbar.) To italicize the text.
7　Update the presentation	

Changing font and font size

Explanation

In addition to applying bold and italic formatting, you can format text by specifying a different font, font size, and font color.

Changing the font

To change the font:

1 Select the text.
2 Using either the Font group or the Mini toolbar, click the Font down-arrow to display the font list.
3 As you point to a font name, a live preview of the font is applied to the selected text.
4 When you decide what font you want to apply, select it.

Changing the font size

To change the font size:

1 Select the text.
2 Using either the Font group or the Mini toolbar, click the Font Size down-arrow to display the font size list.
3 As you point to a font size, a live preview of the font size is applied to the selected text.
4 When you decide what font size you want to apply, select it.

Changing the font color

To change the font color, select the text. Then, in the Font group or on the Mini toolbar, click the Font Color down arrow to display the Font Color gallery. When you select a color, it's applied to the selected text, and the gallery closes. After applying a color, the horizontal line at the bottom of the Font Color button displays that color. You can apply the indicated color to additional text by clicking the button itself, rather than clicking the down arrow.

Do it! **A-2: Changing the font, font size, and font color**

Here's how	Here's why
1 Triple-click **Outlander**	To select the text "Outlander Spices." You'll make the title larger.
2 In the Font group, click the Font down arrow, as shown	

Times New Roma ▼ 44 ▼

B *I* <u>U</u> ~~abc~~ **S** AV ▼

Font

	To display a list of fonts.
Point to a font	Notice that a live preview of the font is applied to the selected text.
Select **Arial Black**	To change the font.
3 Select **Project phase one**	Triple-click any word in the subtitle text.
Activate the Mini toolbar	Point to it.
From the Font list, select **Arial**	To apply the font to the selected text.
4 In the Font group, click the Font Size down arrow, as shown	

Arial ▼ 32 ▼

B *I* <u>U</u> ~~abc~~ **S** AV

Font

	(The subtitle text should still be selected.) To display a list of font sizes.
Select **40**	To increase the font size of the subtitle text.
5 Go to slide 2	(In the Slides tab on the left side of the screen, click the thumbnail for the second slide.) You'll format the slide title.
6 Apply the font **Arial Black** and a font size of **54** to the slide title	Triple-click the slide title text to select it, and use the Font list and Font Size list in the Font group.
7 Verify that **Outlander Spices** is selected	

8	Click as shown	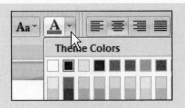
		(The Font Color button is in the Font group.) To display the Font Color gallery.
	Under Standard Colors, select the green color	(Select the color with the ScreenTip that reads "Green," not "Light Green.") To apply the color and close the gallery.
9	Deselect the text	Notice that the text color has changed from black to green.
	Observe the Font Color button	The button shows the last color you selected. You can click the button to apply that color without opening the color gallery.
10	Go to slide 1	In the Slides tab on the left side of the screen, click the thumbnail for the first slide.
11	Select **Outlander Spices**	
	In the Font group, click	(Click the Font Color button, and not the down arrow.) To apply the green color that you used most recently.
12	Update the presentation	

Format Painter

Explanation

You can use the Format Painter button to create consistent text formatting throughout a presentation. It copies the formatting of the selected text, which you can then apply to other text simply by selecting the text you want to format. This button saves you time because it can apply complex formatting options in a single step.

To format text by using the Format Painter:

1   Select the text that contains the formatting you are going to copy.

2   Click the Format Painter button in the Clipboard group or on the Mini toolbar. Notice that the button is locked in the down position and the pointer has changed shape. This is because the pointer is "loaded" with the copied formats.

3   Select the text that you want to apply the copied formatting to. The Format Painter button and the mouse pointer both return to their normal state.

Using the Format Painter multiple times

If you want to use the Format Painter to copy selected formatting multiple times, then you should double-click the Format Painter button to select it, rather than clicking it once. The Format Painter button remains locked in the down position and the pointer remains "loaded" so you can continue selecting text to apply the copied formatting. Click the Format Painter button again or click another option on the PowerPoint window to turn off the Format Painter.

Do it!

A-3: Using the Format Painter to copy text formatting

Here's how	Here's why
1 Go to slide 2	
2 Select **Outlander Spices**	The title of the slide.
3 In the Clipboard group, point to [icon]	(The Format Painter button.) To display the ScreenTip for this button.
Read the ScreenTip	It tells you how to use the Format Painter.
4 Click [icon]	You'll apply the formatting of the selected text to text on another slide.
Observe the Format Painter button	It remains locked in the down position, indicating that it is active.
5 Press (PAGE DOWN)	To move to the next slide.
6 Point to the slide	[icon]
	Notice that the pointer has changed to an I-beam with a paintbrush next to it.
7 Point to the beginning of the word **Project**	(On the third slide.) You'll drag across the text that you want to format.
Drag to select the words **Project justification**	To apply the copied formatting.
8 Observe the selected text	The formatting from the first slide's title is applied to the selected text.
Observe the Format Painter button	It has returned to its normal state, indicating that it is not active.
Deselect the text	(Click outside of the placeholder.) Notice that the pointer has returned to its normal shape.
9 Select **Project justification**	You'll access the Format Painter from the Mini toolbar this time.
Activate the Mini toolbar	
Double-click [icon]	(On the Mini toolbar.) To lock the Format Painter so you can format text multiple times. You'll apply the formatting of the selected text to the title text on multiple slides.

10	Move to the next slide	
	Select **Cost of expansion**	(Drag across the text.) To apply the formatting. Notice that the pointer is still an I-beam with a paintbrush next to it.
11	Apply the formatting to the title text on the remaining slides	
12	Click the **Format Painter** button	(In either the Clipboard group or on the Mini toolbar.) To turn off the feature.
13	Update the presentation	

Changing the bullet style

Explanation

If you want to emphasize a bulleted slide or make a two-level bulleted list stand out, you can change the bullet styles.

To do so, select the text next to the bullet or bullets that you want to change. In the Paragraph group or on the Mini toolbar, click the Bullets down arrow to display the Bullets gallery. Click one of the available bullet styles to apply it and close the gallery.

If you want to remove bullet formatting or apply bullet formatting, then you can select the text and click the Bullets button in the Paragraph group on the Home tab. If you want to demote bulleted or numbered text to a sub-list, you can select the text and do either of the following:

- Press Tab.
- Click the Increase List Level button in the Paragraph group.

When you demote bulleted text, the text is indented to the right, the text size is reduced, and the bullet character changes. When you demote numbered text, the text is indented to the right, the text size is reduced, and the numbering starts over at 1.

If you want to promote bulleted or numbered text to a higher level, then select the text and do either of the following:

- Press Shift+Tab.
- Click the Decrease List Level button in the Paragraph group.

Do it!

A-4: Changing bullet styles

Here's how	Here's why
1 Go to slide 2	You'll change the bullet styles on this slide.
2 Select the text as shown	(Point to the left of "Project" and drag down and to the right.) You'll change the bullet style.
3 In the Paragraph group, click the Bullets down arrow	(Or use the Mini toolbar.) To display the Bullets gallery.
Observe the gallery	By default, the previously applied bullet style is selected.

4 Select the Checkmark Bullets style, as shown	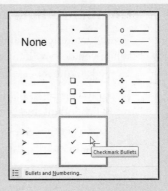
	To apply the new bullet style.
5 Observe the slide	The bullet style changes.
6 Go to slide 3	The two items below "Provide high-quality merchandise" should be indented, because they are a sub-list.
7 Select the third and fourth items	The items that begin with "Work" and "Purchase."

8 Press (TAB)	• Control inventory costs and levels
	• Provide high-quality merchandise
	  – Work with local farmers
	  – Purchase only fresh spices
	• Price merchandise competitively
	• Control cash flow

	To demote the selected items to indicate a sub-list within the larger list.
9 Update the presentation	

Numbered lists

Explanation

Similar to applying bullets to text, you can also apply automatic numbering to a list. When you do, any item you add to the list is numbered sequentially according to the previous number.

To apply numbered list formatting, select the text and click the Numbering button to apply the default numbering style. To apply a specific numbering style:

1 Select the text.

2 In the Paragraph group, click the Numbering down arrow to display the Numbering gallery.

3 Click one of the available numbering styles to apply it and close the gallery.

Do it!

A-5:   Applying a numbered list

Here's how	Here's why
1 Move to the seventh slide	
2 Click within the bulleted text	To place the insertion point.
Press CTRL + A	To select all the text within the placeholder.
3 In the Paragraph group, click	(Click the Numbering button, not the down arrow.) To apply the default numbering style.
Observe the slide	The bulleted list has changed into a numbered list. You'll specify a different numbering style.
4 Click the Numbering down arrow, as shown	To open the Numbering gallery.
5 Click the Number style as shown	Next, you'll add another item to the list.

6	Place the insertion point at the end of the fifth line	Click after the word "program."
	Press ⏎ ENTER	To create a new line.
7	Observe the slide	The new line is numbered accordingly.
8	Type **New employees**	You'll add another item to the list.
	Press ⏎ ENTER	
	Type **Training**	To add a seventh bullet. You'll remove the sixth item.
9	Select the sixth numbered item	Triple-click "New employees."
	Press DELETE	To delete this item from the list.
	Observe the list	The numbering adjusts automatically.
10	Delete the last numbered item	(Triple-click "Training" and press Delete.) The numbered list now has five items in it.
11	Update the presentation	

Topic B: Modifying text

This topic covers the following Microsoft Certified Application Specialist exam objectives for PowerPoint 2007.

#	Objective
2.2.1	Cut, copy, and paste text
	• Move text using drag and drop
	• Copy and paste text
	• Cut and paste text
	• Cut and paste special
2.3.2	Copy elements from one slide to another
	• Copy elements within presentations
	• Copy elements between presentations

Moving and copying text

Explanation

You can move and copy text and objects from one slide to another or from one presentation to another. This can be a significant time saver as you reorganize a presentation. It's also useful if you want to use only a portion of an existing slide in another presentation.

The Find and Replace commands

You can search for all instances of specific text within a presentation and change that text by using the Find and Replace commands. You'll save time because you don't need to read through the entire set of slides to find that text.

To find and replace text:

1. On the Home tab, in the Editing group, click Find to display the Find dialog box.
2. In the Find what box, type the text you want to find.
3. Click Replace to change the dialog box to the Replace dialog box, which includes the Replace with box.
4. In the Replace with box, type the text you want to use.
5. Click Find Next to start the search. PowerPoint will highlight the first occurrence of the found text.
6. Click Replace if you want to change a single occurrence, or click Replace All if you want to change all occurrences of that specific text.

Do it!

B-1: Finding and replacing text

Here's how	Here's why
1 Move to the first slide	
2 On the Home tab, in the Editing group, click **Find**	To open the Find dialog box. The insertion point appears in the Find what box.
3 In the Find what box, type **merchandise**	You'll replace the word "merchandise" with the word "products."
4 Verify that Match case is cleared	To ensure that the search locates the word whether or not it is capitalized.
5 Click **Replace**	To change the dialog box to the Replace dialog box, which includes the Replace with box.
6 In the Replace with box, type **products**	
7 Click **Find Next**	The first instance of the word "merchandise" is highlighted in the presentation.
8 Click **Replace**	To change the selected word to "products." The next instance of the word "merchandise" is selected.
9 Click **Replace**	To replace the second instance of "merchandise" to "products." A message box appears, indicating that the search is complete.
Click **OK**	To close the message box.
10 Click **Close**	To close the Replace dialog box.
Deselect the text	
11 Update the presentation	

The Cut and Paste commands

Explanation

When you want to move text or an object from one location to another, you use the Cut command. The Cut command removes the text or object from its original location so you can paste it elsewhere. When the Cut command removes text or an object from a slide, it places it on the Clipboard.

The Clipboard

When you move or copy text or objects, PowerPoint places the selected text or object on the Clipboard. The *Clipboard* is a temporary storage area that holds the text or object until you specify where to place it in a document. The Clipboard can hold only one selection at a time and is cleared when you shut down your computer. You can overcome this limitation by using the Clipboard task pane, which can hold up to 24 individual items on it.

After you use the Cut command to move text or an object to the Clipboard, you can place the text or object in a new location on the same slide, on another slide, or in a different presentation altogether. To place an item, you use the Paste command. The *Paste* command takes the text or object from the Clipboard and inserts a copy of it wherever the insertion point is positioned.

To move text or an object:

1 Select the text or object that you want to move.
2 In the Clipboard group, click the Cut button, or press Ctrl+X.
3 Place the insertion point wherever you want to insert the text or object. This can be on the same slide, another slide, or in another presentation.
4 In the Clipboard group, click the Paste button or press Ctrl+V.

Paste Special

When you copy text from one slide to another, the text appears on the new slide with the formatting it displayed on the original slide. However, you can use the Paste Special command to specify that the text is pasted as unformatted text, so that it appears using the formatting of the new slide. To paste text as unformatted text:

1 Place the insertion point where you want to paste the text.
2 In the Clipboard group, click Paste to display the Paste menu.
3 Choose Paste Special to open the Paste Special dialog box.
4 In the As list, select Unformatted Text and click OK.

Drag and drop

You can also move text by using drag and drop. To drag and drop text to a new location:

1 Select the text you want to move.
2 Point to the selected text. The pointer appears as an arrow.
3 Press and hold the mouse button, and drag to move the text to a new location on the slide.
4 Release the mouse button to move the text to the new location.

Do it!   **B-2: Cutting and dragging text**

Here's how	Here's why
1 Go to slide 6	The last item in the list on this slide has not yet been accomplished, so you'll move it to the "Outstanding issues" slide. You're moving a bulleted item to a numbered list, so you must be careful to select only the text, and not the entire paragraph, which includes the bullet formatting.
2 Point just before the word **Specifications** and click	To place the insertion point to the left of the word. You'll use the Shift-click method to select the text.
Point just after the word **initiative**	(Point to the right of the letter "e" at the end of the word so that the pointer touches the "e.") You need to be sure not to select any blank space after the word.
Press (SHIFT) and click	To select the text without including any blank space after the text. Selecting the space to the right of the last word would cause the entire line to be selected, including the bullet character formatting.
3 In the Clipboard group, click ✂	(The Cut button.) To remove the text from the slide and place it on the Clipboard.
4 Press (← BACKSPACE) twice	To remove the leftover bullet character and blank line.
5 Go to the last slide	
6 Click at the end of the last line	To place the insertion point.
Press (↵ ENTER)	To add a sixth item to the list.
7 On the Clipboard group, click the **Paste** button	
	(Click the top portion of the button, not the down arrow.) To paste the text from the Clipboard to the numbered list. The text is pasted with its blue formatting. You'll undo this step and use Paste Special to paste the text without its original formatting.
8 Click ↶ ▾	(The Undo button is on the Quick Access toolbar.) To undo the paste step.
9 Click the **Paste** down arrow	To display the Paste menu.
Choose **Paste Special...**	To open the Paste Special dialog box.

10 In the As list, scroll to the bottom	
Select **Unformatted Text**	
Click **OK**	To paste the text without its original formatting. The pasted text automatically takes on the formatting of the paragraph in which you pasted it.
11 Press ⏎ ENTER	To add a blank line below the item you just pasted. You'll move the third item to the end of the list by dragging it.
12 Triple-click **Building**	To select "Building a Web site."
13 Point to the selected text	The pointer appears as a white arrow, indicating that you can drag to move the text.
14 Press and hold the mouse button and drag to the empty line	To move the selected text to the end of the list. The item numbering is updated automatically.
15 Update the presentation	

The Copy command

Explanation

When you want to copy text or an object from one location to another, you use the Copy command. The *Copy* command creates a copy of the selected text or object on the Clipboard. This is different from the Cut command because the Copy command does not remove the selected text or object from its original location. However, you still use the Paste command to complete the copy procedure.

To copy text or an object:

1   Select the text or object that you want to copy.

2   In the Clipboard group, click the Copy button or press Ctrl+C.

3   Place the insertion point wherever you want to insert the text or object. This can be on the same slide, another slide, or in another presentation.

4   On the Clipboard group, click the Paste button or press Ctrl+V.

The Paste Options button

The text you paste might be formatted differently than the text in the location where you want to paste it. You can choose whether to keep the text formatting as it is or inherit the formatting of the destination paragraph by using the Paste Options button, which appears to the right of any text you've pasted. To use the Paste Options button, click the down arrow and select the relevant formatting option.

Do it!

B-3: Copying text to another slide

Here's how	Here's why
1 At the end of the presentation, insert a new slide	Move to the last slide and click the New Slide button. Verify that the Title and Content slide layout is applied.
2 Go to slide 2	
Select **Outlander Spices**	Triple-click the text to select the entire line.
3 In the Clipboard group, click 🗎	(The Copy button.) To copy the title to the Clipboard. The text also remains in its original location.
Go to the last slide	
4 Click the title placeholder	To place the insertion point.
On the Clipboard group, click the **Paste** button	(Click the top portion of the button, not the down arrow.) To paste the text from the Clipboard to the title placeholder.
5 Observe the slide	The title text is inserted from the Clipboard. Notice that the Paste Options button appears on the slide.
6 Click as shown	
	To display the Paste Options menu.
Choose **Keep Source Formatting**	The pasted text has the same formatting as the source text.
7 Deselect the title placeholder	Next, you'll copy text from one slide and paste it on a slide in another presentation.
8 Go to slide 5	You'll copy the text in the left text box.
9 Copy the text in the left text box	(Click the left text box, and press Ctrl+A. Click the Copy button.) You'll paste the text in a new presentation.
10 Create a blank new presentation	Click the Office button and choose New. Select Blank Presentation and click Create.
11 Create a new slide	Click the top portion of the New Slide button.
12 Click within the content placeholder	To place the insertion point.
Paste the text	Click the top portion of the Paste button.

13 Save the presentation as **My pasted text**	In the current unit folder.
14 Close the presentation	You return to the My project phase one presentation.
15 Update the presentation	

The Clipboard pane

Explanation

In addition to the standard Clipboard, you can also use the Clipboard pane. These features differ in that the Clipboard pane can store multiple items and is integrated across all Office programs. Because of this expanded capacity, you can use it to copy multiple items in succession and then paste them, one at a time or simultaneously, into the preferred location(s) in your presentation. This procedure is called *collect and paste*. Because this tool is integrated across Office 2007, you can use it in any Office program, such as Word, Excel, Outlook, Access, or PowerPoint.

To use the collect and paste procedure, you must use the Clipboard pane, which you can display by clicking the Dialog Box Launcher at the bottom-right corner of the Clipboard group.

Collect and paste

When you collect and paste multiple items, the items can come from any program that has the Copy command. After copying the items, you can paste the collected items into your other Office 2007 programs by using the Clipboard pane. For example, you can copy a chart in Excel, switch to Word and copy part of a document, switch to Internet Explorer and copy some text, and then switch to PowerPoint and paste the collected items in any order.

To copy an item to the Office Clipboard, select the item and use the standard copy procedures (such as pressing Ctrl+C).

The Clipboard pane

The objects that you copy by using the Office Clipboard appear in the Clipboard pane. The Clipboard pane can contain a maximum of 24 copied items. The contents of the Clipboard pane are not cleared when you close the pane. To clear the contents of the task pane, you use the Clear All button.

The following table describes the options on the Clipboard pane.

Option	Description
Paste All	Pastes all of the collected items simultaneously at the insertion point. The items are pasted in the order in which they were collected.
Clear All	Clears the contents of the Clipboard pane.
Paste	Pastes the selected item at the insertion point.
Delete	Clears the selected item from the Clipboard pane.

Do it!

B-4:   Using the Clipboard pane

Here's how	Here's why
1 At the end of the presentation, insert a new slide	Use the default Title and Content layout.
2 Type **Summary** as the title of the new slide	
3 In the Clipboard group, click the Dialog Box Launcher, as shown	
	To display the Clipboard pane. It contains the text that you pasted to the new presentation.
4 Click ⌧ Clear All	(The Clear All button is on the Clipboard pane.) To clear the Clipboard.
5 Move to the third slide	You'll copy contents from this slide.
6 Copy the first two items from the bullet list	(Drag to select the two items; then click the Copy button in the Clipboard group.) The Clipboard pane now contains the copied text. The Clipboard pane also shows that this is the first item out of 24 items that you can copy.
7 Move to the sixth slide	You'll copy contents from this slide as well.
8 Copy the first two items from the bullet list	The Clipboard pane now contains both items of copied text. The most recently copied text becomes the first item in the Clipboard pane's list. The Clipboard pane also shows that this is the second item out of 24 items you can copy.
9 Move to the last slide	The slide you just created.
10 Place the insertion point in the content placeholder	
11 In the Clipboard pane, point to the top item	(Do not click.) To display the item's down arrow. From the down arrow, you can choose Paste or Delete. You an also paste an item by clicking the item.
12 Click the top item	(In the Clipboard pane.) The slide now contains the bullet items copied from the sixth slide.
Press ↵ ENTER	(If necessary.) To create a blank bulleted line below the two items you pasted.

13	Paste the second item from the Clipboard pane	Point to the second item on the Clipboard pane, click the down-arrow and choose Paste.
14	Clear the contents of the Clipboard pane	Click the Clear All button on the Clipboard pane.
	Click as shown	
		To close the Clipboard pane.
15	Press (← BACKSPACE) twice	(If necessary.) To remove the extra bullet and line.
16	Apply a black color to all the text	Press Ctrl+A; then click the Font Color button's down arrow and select a black swatch.
17	Update the presentation	

Topic C: Paragraph formatting

This topic covers the following Microsoft Certified Application Specialist exam objective for PowerPoint 2007.

#	Objective
2.2.6	Format paragraphs
	• Align text
	• Change line spacing
	• Change indentation

Paragraph formatting examples

Explanation

Text alignment, text spacing, and indentation are considered paragraph formatting, because they always apply to an entire paragraph. To adjust any type of paragraph formatting, you can select any part of a paragraph, or you can simply place the insertion point within the paragraph.

Text alignment

When text uses *Align Left* formatting, the lines of text are aligned along the left side of the text placeholder, and the right side of the paragraph appears ragged. When text uses *Align Right* formatting, the lines of text are aligned along the right side of the text placeholder, and the left side looks ragged. You can *Justify* text so that the lines end evenly at the left and right sides of the placeholder.

To align text, place the insertion point in a line of text, or select multiple paragraphs. In the Paragraph group, click the Align Left, Center, Align Right, or Justify button. You can also use the alignment buttons on the Mini toolbar. In addition, you can specify alignment settings by using the Paragraph dialog box.

Line spacing

You can format line spacing to adjust the space between lines of text. To adjust line spacing, place the insertion point in a line of text, or select multiple paragraphs, and then in the Paragraph group click the Line Spacing button and choose a line spacing value. Line spacing values are measured in lines. You can also add space before or after a paragraph. To do so:

1 Open the Paragraph dialog box using either of these techniques:

• Click the Line Spacing button and choose More.

• In the Paragraph group, click the Dialog Box Launcher.

2 Under Spacing, enter a value in the Before or After box. You also can use the Line Spacing list to select a line spacing value.

3 Click OK.

Text indentation

You can also use the Paragraph dialog box to specify paragraph indentation. To indent the left side of all lines of a paragraph, you can enter a value in the Before box. You also can specify a first-line indent value or a hanging indent value. If you don't want a first-line indent or a hanging indent, then select (none) from the list of indenting styles. After specifying text indent settings, click OK.

Do it!

C-1: Applying paragraph formatting

Here's how	Here's why
1 Move to the fifth slide in the presentation	The slide titled "Performance."
Select the left-side text	The text on the left is in its own placeholder. You'll change the alignment of the entire left side of the slide.
2 Click ▤	(The Align Right button is in the Paragraph group.) To align the text to the right.
Deselect and observe the text	**Performance** Our pricing typically undercuts our competitors', yet still provides a large margin of profit for distributors. Our products are manufactured for quality, and have earned end-user loyalty resulting in repeat sales. Our products move! Inventory typically turns over 50% faster than competitive products. Our customers have saved up to 14% of inventory cost while improving productivity and cash flow. Sales to restaurants have never been better.
	The left-side text is aligned to the right, and the right-side text is still aligned to the left.
3 Select the left-side text again	
4 Activate the Mini toolbar	Right-click the selected text to display the Mini toolbar.
Click ▤	(The Center button is on the Mini toolbar and in the Paragraph group.) To align the left-side text to the center.

5 Align the right-side text to the center	Select the text, and click the Center button.
Deselect the text	
Observe the slide	

Both text blocks have centered text.

6 Align the left-side text to the left	
Align the right-side text to the left	Next, you'll increase the line spacing. To format both text boxes at the same time, you'll select them both.
7 Click the left text box	To select it.
Press and hold (SHIFT) and click the right text box	To select both text boxes.
8 Click	The Line Spacing button is in the Paragraph group.
Choose **1.5**	To increase the line spacing.
9 Go to slide 3	You'll increase the left indent for the sub-list.
10 Select the two items in the sub-list	
11 In the Paragraph group, click the Dialog Box Launcher	To open the Paragraph dialog box.
12 Under Indentation, in the Before text box, enter **1**	To specify a left indent of 1 inch.
Click **OK**	To close the Paragraph dialog box.
13 Update and close the presentation	

Unit summary: Formatting slides

Topic A   In this topic, you applied **character formatting**, such as bold and italic, to selected text by using commands in the Font group and Mini toolbar. You also changed the **font** and **font size**. You used the **Format Painter** to repeat text formatting. Then, you changed **bulleted styles** and applied a **numbered list**.

Topic B   In this topic, you used the **Find** dialog box to search for specific text, and you used the **Replace** dialog box to replace text. Next, you used the **Cut**, **Copy**, and **Paste** commands to move text to another slide in the same presentation and to another presentation. You also dragged text to move it. Finally, you used the **Clipboard pane** to copy and paste multiple items.

Topic C   In this topic, you applied **paragraph formatting** such as text alignment, line spacing, and indentation.

Independent practice activity

In this activity, you'll search for specific text and replace it. You'll apply formatting to text, and you'll use the Format Painter to repeat that formatting.

1　Open New activities practice (from the current unit folder).

2　Save the presentation as **My new activities practice**.

3　Find the text **Creating** and replace it with the word **Developing**.

4　Find the phrase **Markets in the East** and replace it with the phrase **Markets in the North**.

5　Apply bold formatting to the first slide's title, and increase the font size to 60.

6　On the second slide, format the title as Trebuchet MS, Bold, and apply a red color. Align the title to the left.

7　Using the Format Painter, apply this formatting to the titles of the remaining slides. (*Hint*: After applying the formatting, remember to disable the Format Painter.)

8　On the second slide, apply a new bullet style. Using the Format Painter, apply this change to the other bulleted lists in the presentation.

9　Update and close the presentation.

Review questions

1 What is the difference between character formatting and paragraph formatting?

2 List the buttons in the Font group.

3 What is the Mini toolbar?

4 List the steps you would use to apply a new font to slide text.

5 You can use the _____ button to copy the formatting of the selected text, and then apply it to other text.

6 How can you change the bullet style for a selected bullet list on a slide?

7 What is the Clipboard?

8 How do you open the Find dialog box?

9 What do the Cut and Paste commands do?

10 How does the Clipboard pane differ from the Clipboard?

11 You select one entire paragraph and part of another, and then click the Center button. What happens to the text?

Unit 4

Drawing objects

Unit time: 60 minutes

Complete this unit, and you'll know how to:

A Draw objects by using tools in the Drawing group.

B Format, modify, move, rotate, and delete drawn objects by using groups on the Drawing Tools Format tab.

C Add text to drawn objects and add text to text boxes.

Topic A: Shapes

This topic covers the following Microsoft Certified Application Specialist exam objective for PowerPoint 2007.

#	Objective
3.3.2	Insert shapes

Shapes in presentations

Explanation

You can make your presentations more appealing by adding drawn objects, such as rectangles, ovals, lines, arrows, and other shapes. The tools needed to draw objects are located on the Insert tab and on the Drawing Tools Format tab, which is context sensitive.

Drawing shapes

To create an object on a slide:

1   Activate the Home tab.

2   In the Drawing group, click Shapes to display the Shapes gallery and select one of the available tools, such as the Rectangle tool shown in Exhibit 4-1. You can also access the Shapes gallery in the Illustrations group on the Insert tab.

3   Point to the location where you want to begin drawing. The pointer changes to a crosshair.

4   Drag until the drawing object reaches the size and shape you want.

5   Release the mouse button. The object is automatically selected.

Another way to create an object is to select a tool and click the slide. The specified shape is automatically drawn at a default size.

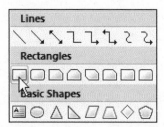

Exhibit 4-1: The Rectangle tool located in the Shapes gallery

Exhibit 4-2 shows a selected drawn object and identifies the parts of it. You use the rotate handle to change the rotation angle and the sizing handles to resize the object.

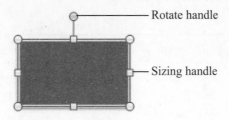

Exhibit 4-2: A drawn object

Polygons

When you select a polygon, it might display one or more yellow *adjustment handles* in addition to the rotate handle and sizing handles. You can drag an adjustment handle to reshape the shape. When you point to an adjustment handle, the pointer appears as a white arrowhead, as shown in Exhibit 4-3.

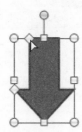

Exhibit 4-3: The pointer as it appears when pointing to an adjustment handle

Contextual Tool feature

When you select a drawn object, Microsoft's Context Tool feature will add the Drawing Tools Format tab to the Ribbon, as shown in Exhibit 4-4. This tab contains the options you'll need to format the object.

Exhibit 4-4: The Drawing Tools Format tab

Microsoft Office 2007's new Context Tool feature will automatically display the appropriate tab when you insert a picture, create a text box, draw a chart, or draw a diagram. You can then activate the tab to work with it.

Do it!

A-1: Using the drawing tools

Here's how	Here's why
1 Create a new blank presentation	Click the Office button and choose New. In the New Presentation dialog box, click Blank Presentation and click Create.
2 In the title placeholder, enter **Drawing Practice**	To give the presentation a name.
3 Click the **New Slide** down arrow	(In the Slides group.) To display the slide layout gallery. You'll select the Blank layout.
4 Select the **Blank** layout	(Scroll down in the slide layout gallery, and click Blank.) To create a new blank slide.
5 Save the presentation as **My drawing practice**	In the current unit folder.
6 Click **Shapes** and click as shown	(On the Home tab, in the Drawing group.) To select the Rectangle tool.
Point to the slide	
Observe the pointer	It appears as a crosshair.
7 Drag to create a rectangle, as shown	The rectangle should be roughly one quarter the width of the slide.
Release the mouse button	To complete the rectangle.

8 Observe the rectangle

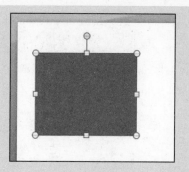

The default fill (blue) is applied to it. It has four corner sizing handles, four side sizing handles, and a rotate handle.

Observe the Ribbon

The Drawing Tools Format tab automatically appears. After you draw an object, insert a picture, create a text box, draw a chart, or draw a diagram, a tab appears in the Ribbon that you can activate to format the object.

9 Click a blank part of the slide

(To deselect the rectangle.) The Drawing Tools Format tab no longer appears in the Ribbon.

10 Select the rectangle

11 Activate the Drawing Tools Format tab

12 In the Insert Shapes group, click as shown

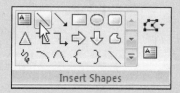

To select the Line tool.

13 Press and hold (SHIFT)

To constrain the line you'll draw to be vertical, horizontal, or at a 45-degree angle.

Point above and to the left of the rectangle and drag to the right

Pressing Shift ensured that the line was drawn perfectly horizontally.

14 Press (DELETE)

To delete the line.

15	Draw an arrow above the rectangle that points to the rectangle	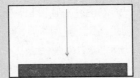
		On the Home tab, click Shapes, and select the Arrow tool. Point above the rectangle, press and hold Shift, and drag down. Click a blank area to deselect the arrow.
16	Delete the arrow	(Select the arrow and press Delete.) You'll draw a block arrow.
17	Select the **Down Arrow** tool	On the Home tab, click Shapes, and under Block Arrows, select the Down Arrow tool.
18	Point above the rectangle, and begin dragging down and to the right	(Don't release the mouse button.) Dragging horizontally adjusts the shape's width, and dragging vertically adjusts its height.
	Drag to specify the arrow size and dimensions; then release the mouse button	
19	Delete the shape	Press Delete.
20	Update the presentation	

Switching object shapes

Explanation

After you draw an object, you can change it to a different shape. For example, after drawing a rectangle, you can change it to an oval. To change an object to another shape:

1 Select the existing shape you want to change.
2 Verify that the Drawing Tools Format tab is activated.
3 In the Insert Shapes group, click the Edit Shape down arrow and point to Change Shape to display the gallery.
4 Select the shape you want to use. The new shape replaces the old one, but retains any formatting you had applied to the old shape.

Do it!

A-2: Switching the object shape

Here's how	Here's why
1 Select the rectangle	You'll change the rectangle to an oval.
2 Activate the Drawing Tools Format tab	
3 In the Insert Shapes group, click the Edit Shape down arrow	
	To display the Edit Shape menu.
4 Point to **Change Shape**	To display the gallery.
5 Under Basic Shapes, click the Oval shape	To change the shape of the rectangle to an oval.
6 Update the presentation	

Topic B: Modifying objects

This topic covers the following Microsoft Certified Application Specialist exam objectives for PowerPoint 2007.

#	Objective
3.4.1	Apply Quick Styles to shapes and pictures
	• Apply fill to shapes
	• Remove borders from shapes
3.5.1	Size, scale, and rotate illustrations and other content
	• Adjust size
	• Adjust scale
	• Adjust rotation
3.5.3	Group and align illustrations and other content
3.5.4	Use gridlines and guides to arrange illustrations and other content

Formatting objects

Explanation

When you create objects, you can change fill colors, outline colors, and effects. You can make the changes quickly by using options in the Shape Styles group. You can also duplicate, move, resize, rotate, and change shapes. If you no longer need a drawn object, you can delete it.

Shape styles

The Drawing Tools Format tab includes the Shape Styles group. It contains the Shape Fill, Shape Outline, and Shape Effects buttons that you can use to modify an object manually. It also displays Shape Styles that you can use to quickly apply a complete set of fill color, outline color, and effects. When you point to one of the styles, a live preview is displayed on the selected object(s). To access more of the shape styles, click the More down arrow to display a gallery of available styles. Point to one of the styles to view the live preview, or select it to apply that style.

Shape Fills

To change an object's fill color, select the object and activate the Drawing Tools Format tab. In the Shape Styles group, click the Shape Fill down arrow to display its contents. Select a color to make the change. The following table describes the options available in the Shape Fill list.

Option	Description
Theme Colors	Contains ten main colors and five tints under each main color (for a total of 60 color swatches).
Standard Colors	Contains the ten regular colors that span the color spectrum, including: Dark Red, Red, Orange, Yellow, Light Green, Green, Light Blue, Blue, Dark Blue, and Purple
No Fill	Removes the fill completely.
More Fill Colors	Opens the Colors dialog box, which contains two tabs: the Standard tab and the Custom tab. On the Custom tab, you can change the color model, change the color tint, change the Transparency, and select any of the millions of colors that are available.
Picture	Opens the Insert Picture dialog box, which you can use to add an image file as a fill.
Gradient	Opens a gallery of gradients divided into two categories, Light Variations and Dark Variations.
Texture	Opens a gallery of 24 textured fills.

Shape outlines

To change an object's outline color, select the object. In the Shape Styles group, click the Shape Outlines down arrow to display its contents. Select a color to make the change or use one of the other options, such as No Outline, More Outline Colors, Weight, Dashes, and Arrows.

Shape effects

To change the effects applied to a shape, select the object. In the Shape Styles group, click the Shape Effects down arrow to display its contents. You can use the Preset, Shadow, Reflection, Glow, Soft Edges, Bevel, and 3-D Rotation submenu items to display the respective galleries. From the desired gallery, select an effect to apply.

Do it!

B-1: Applying formatting to objects

Here's how	Here's why
1 Verify that the oval is selected and the Drawing Tools Format tab is activated	Click the oval to select it and activate the Drawing Tools Format tab.
2 In the Shape Styles group, point to the second style	 To see the live preview applied to the object.
Click the first style	(In the Shape Styles group.) To apply the style to the object.
3 In the Shape Styles group, click the More down arrow as shown	 To display a gallery with more styles.
Click the Colored Fill – Accent 3 style	 Use the ScreenTips to identify the styles.
4 Observe the oval	(Without deselecting it.) The fill color changes and an outline color is applied.
5 In the Shape Styles group, click the **Shape Fill** down arrow	To display the available fill colors and fill options.
Observe the Shape Fill list	It contains Theme Colors and Standard Colors that you can apply by clicking one. To see more colors, select More Fill Colors. You can set the shape to have no fill, or you can add a gradient or a texture to it. In addition, you can add an image file to an object.
Under Theme Colors, select Red, Accent 2	(Red, Accent 2 is in the first row under Theme Colors.) The fill color changes.

6 Click the **Shape Outline** down arrow	To display the available outline colors and options.
Observe the Shape Outline list	You can apply a color quickly to the shape outline by clicking one of the Theme Colors or Standard Colors. To see more colors, choose More Outline Colors. You can set the shape to have no outline, change the line weight, apply dashes, and add an arrow or two.
Click the **Shape Outline** down arrow	To close the list without changing the shape outline.
7 Click the **Shape Effects** down arrow	To display the available effects options.
Point to each effect submenu	To see the available galleries.
Point to **Preset**	To display the gallery of options. Currently, no 3-D effect is applied.
Under Presets, select Preset 2	(The second item in t1he first row.) To apply the new effect.
8 Update the presentation	

Duplicating objects

After you create an object, you can duplicate it. Creating duplicates ensures that similar objects have a uniform size and shape in your presentation. For example, if your presentation contains multiple oval objects, you can make them all the same by creating duplicates of the original oval.

To duplicate an object:

1   Select the object.
2   Activate the Home tab.
3   In the Clipboard group, click the Paste down arrow and choose Duplicate.

You can also press Ctrl+D to duplicate a selected object.

Deleting objects

To remove an object that is no longer needed, select it and press Delete.

Moving objects

After an object is drawn or duplicated, you'll probably want to move it. To do so:

1   Select the object. The rotate handle and sizing handles appear around it.
2   Point to the object:
    • If the object has a fill applied to it, point anywhere on the object and the mouse pointer displays a four-headed arrow.
    • If the object doesn't have a fill (no color and completely empty), point to the edge of the selected object but not to any of the sizing handles. The mouse pointer displays a four-headed arrow.
3   Drag the object to move it to a new position.
4   Release the mouse button.

B-2:   Duplicating, deleting, and moving objects

Here's how	Here's why
1 Verify that the oval is selected Activate the Home tab	
2 Copy the oval to the Clipboard	In the Clipboard group, click the Copy button or press Ctrl+C.
3 Paste the oval	In the Clipboard group, click the Paste button or press Ctrl+V.
Observe the ovals	The original is deselected. The pasted copy is offset to the right and down a bit.
4 Verify that the new oval is selected	
5 Press (DELETE)	To delete the oval. No objects are selected.

6 Click the **Paste** down arrow	To display the menu.
Observe the menu	Notice that Duplicate is not available. It is grayed out because no items are selected.
7 Select the oval	The Drawing Tools Format tab is visible but not active.
Click the **Paste** down arrow	Duplicate is now available.
Choose **Duplicate**	To create a duplicate of the oval.
8 Point to the oval	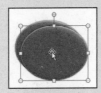
	The pointer changes shape to include a four-pointed arrow, which you are going to use to move the oval.
Click and hold and drag to the right	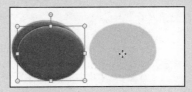
	A transparent preview of the oval moves with the pointer.
Release the mouse button	
	To complete the move.
9 With the oval selected, press ⌈CTRL⌋ + ⌈D⌋	To duplicate it.
Move the third oval to the right	
	(If necessary.) The three ovals are now in a line.

10	Verify that the third oval is selected	
11	Activate the Drawing Tools Format tab	
	In the Shape Styles group, click the **More down** arrow	To display more styles.
	Select the second style	(Colored Outline – Accent 1.) To change the style applied to the object. The fill has been changed to white, and a blue outline has been added.
12	Drag the selected oval to the left	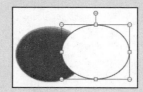
		So that it partially overlaps the oval next to it. You can see the oval's white fill covering the other oval where they overlap.
13	Click the Shape Fill down arrow	You will remove the white fill from the oval.
	Choose **No Fill**	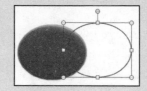
		To remove the fill from the object.

14 Point within the selected oval

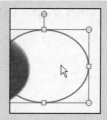

Because there is no longer a fill applied to the object, you can't move it by dragging from within the object.

Point to the shape outline

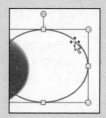

The pointer changes shape to indicate that you can now move the object.

15 Drag to the right and release the mouse button

To move the oval so that it no longer overlaps the other oval.

16 Update the presentation

Resizing objects

Explanation

After drawing an object, you can change its size at any time.

To resize an object:

1 Select the object. The rotate handle and sizing handles appear around it.

2 Point to one of the following:

- Point to one of the corner sizing handles if you want to increase the width and height of the object proportionally. The pointer changes to a diagonal double-headed arrow.

- Point to one of the side sizing handles if you want to increase only the width of an object. The pointer changes to a horizontal double-headed arrow.

- Point to either the top or bottom sizing handle if you want to adjust only the height of an object. The pointer changes to a vertical double-headed arrow.

3 Drag the sizing handle until the object reaches the size you want.

4 Release the mouse button.

If you want to resize an object to a specific numeric value, you can enter values in the Height and Width boxes in the Size group on the Drawing Tools Format tab.

Do it!

B-3:   Resizing an object

Here's how	Here's why
1 Activate the Home tab	
2 Click the **New Slide** down arrow	To display the gallery
Click **Title Only**	To add a new slide with the Title Only layout.
3 In the Title placeholder, enter **Monthly Sales Awards**	You'll create star shapes to contain the names of several employees.
4 In the Drawing group, click **Shapes**	To display the Shapes gallery.
5 Under Stars and Banners, select the 16-Point Star	You'll use this tool to draw a star object.
6 Drag as shown	
	To draw a star of any size.
Release the mouse button	To finish drawing the star. The star is selected, and the Drawing Tools Format tab appears.

7 Point to the bottom-right corner sizing handle, as shown

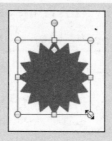

The pointer changes to a diagonal two-way arrow, indicating that you can use it to resize the object's width and height.

Drag down and to the right about an inch

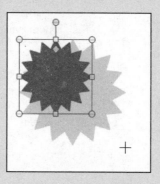

To resize the object's height and width.

Release the mouse button

To finish resizing.

8 Point to the bottom center sizing handle, as shown

The pointer changes to a vertical two-way arrow, indicating you can use it to resize the object by changing the object's height only.

Drag up about half an inch

(Release the mouse button when done.) To reduce the height of the star about half an inch.

9 Point to the center sizing handle on the right side as shown

Drag to the left about half an inch

To reduce the width of the star about half and inch.

10 Activate the Drawing Tools
    Format tab and observe the Size
    group

You'll use this group to resize the star using an
exact measurement. The Height and Width
numbers will vary based on how you've drawn
and resized the star.

11 Point to the Height box

The Height box is at the top of the Size group.
You'll change the height to 2.5 inches.

    Click the current value

To select the value in the Height box.

    Type **2.5**

12 Press ⏎ ENTER

To change the height. You'll change the width
to 2.5 inches.

13 Select the value in the Width box
    and type **2.5**

    Press ⏎ ENTER

To change the width.

14 Update the presentation

Rotating objects

Explanation

You also can change the rotation angle of an object. To rotate an object:

1. Select the object. The rotate handle and sizing handles appear.
2. Point to the Rotate handle. The pointer shape changes to a black circle with an arrow, indicating a rotating motion.
3. Drag either in a clockwise or counter-clockwise motion.
4. Release the mouse button to finish the rotation.

If you want to rotate an object at a specific angle, select an object and verify that the Drawing Tools Format tab is active. In the Size group, click the Dialog Box Launcher to open the Size and Position dialog box. Under Size and rotate, enter the correct angle in the Rotation box and click Close.

Do it!

B-4:   Rotating an object

Here's how	Here's why
1 Point to the Rotation handle as shown	
	The pointer changes shape to a black circle with an arrow, indicating a rotating motion.
Drag down and to the right as shown	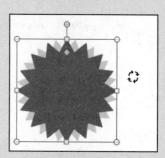
	(And release the mouse button.) To rotate the star to the right.
Observe the star	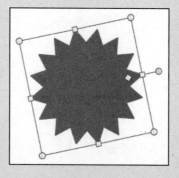
	The star and the selection box are rotated to the right. Notice that the Rotation handle is now at the same angle where the pointer was when you release the mouse button.

2 In the Size group, click the Dialog Box Launcher

(On the Drawing Tools Format tab.) To open the Size and Position dialog box with the Size tab activated.

Observe the Rotation box

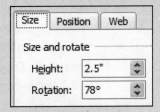

It shows the shape's current rotation. The number in the box will differ based on where you stopped rotating the object.

In the Rotation box, enter **0**

This will return the star back to its original rotation.

Click **Close**

To apply the rotation and close the dialog box.

3 Update the presentation

Aligning objects

Explanation

When placing multiple objects on a slide, it can be difficult to align them to one another by dragging them. Instead, you can use the Align menu to align them in relation to one another and to evenly space them. To align objects:

1   Select one of the objects that you want to align.
2   Press Ctrl or Shift, and select the other objects.
3   Activate the Drawing Tools Format tab.
4   In the Arrange group, click the Align button and choose an option.

The following table explains the options that are available in the Align menu.

Option	Description
Align Left	Aligns the selected objects with the left side of the leftmost object.
Align Center	Aligns the selected objects at their centers.
Align Right	Aligns the selected objects with the right side of the rightmost object.
Align Top	Aligns the selected objects with the top of the topmost object.
Align Middle	Aligns the selected objects at their middles.
Align Bottom	Aligns the selected objects with the bottom of the bottommost object.
Distribute Horizontally	Evenly distributes the horizontal space between the selected objects.
Distribute Vertically	Evenly distributes the vertical space between the selected objects.
Align to Slide	When this option is checked, the Align commands align objects to the slide, rather than to one another.
Align selected objects	When this option is checked, the Align commands align objects to one another, rather than to the slide.
View Gridlines	Displays the default Gridlines on the slide.
Grid Settings	Opens the Grid and Guidelines dialog box.

Grids and guides

When moving objects on a slide, you can use gridlines and guides to place them in exactly the right place. A *grid* is a set of intersecting lines that appear on a slide, as shown in Exhibit 4-5. To display the grid on a slide, verify that the Drawing Tools Format tab is active. In the Arrange group, click the Align button and choose View Gridlines.

A *guide* is a pair of horizontal and vertical nonprinting lines that intersect the middle of the slide by default. They are movable, and you can use them to position objects at specific locations on a slide or to place objects in relation to other objects. To display and use the guides:

1   In the Arrange group, click the Align button and choose Grid Settings to open the Grid and Guides dialog box.
2   Under Guide settings, check Display drawing guides on screen.
3   Click OK.
4   Drag the guide to a position where you want to align the objects.
5   Drag the object near the guide so that the object's center or edge aligns with the guide automatically.

Exhibit 4-5: A slide with a grid and guides

Do it!

B-5: Aligning objects

Here's how	Here's why
1 Select the star object	If necessary.
2 Duplicate the object twice	Press Ctrl+D twice to create two copies.
Move the stars as shown	
3 Press and hold (CTRL) and select the other two star objects	All three objects are now selected.
Release (CTRL)	
4 Activate the Drawing Tools Format tab	If necessary.
Click [icon]	(The Align button is in the Arrange group.) To display the Align menu.
Choose **Distribute Horizontally**	To evenly distribute the horizontal space between the objects.
5 Click the Align button and choose **Align Middle**	To align the three objects based on the middle points of each.
6 Click the Align button and choose **Grid Settings...**	To open the Grid and Guides dialog box.
Under Grid settings, check **Display grid on screen**	
Under Guide settings, check **Display drawing guides on screen**	
Click **OK**	To turn on the grid and guides, and close the dialog box.
7 Observe the slide	The grid and guides have been applied to the slide.

8   Verify that all three shapes are
    selected

    Press ⬆ multiple times | To position the three star objects near the center of the slide. Use the grid and guides as references to determine the slide's center.

9   Open the Grid and Guides dialog
    box | Display the Align menu and choose Grid settings.

    Clear **Display grid on screen**

    Clear **Display drawing
    guides on screen**

    Click **OK** | To remove the grid and guides from the slide, and close the dialog box.

10 Deselect objects | Click the slide.

11 Update the presentation

Topic C: Text in objects

This topic covers the following Microsoft Certified Application Specialist exam objectives for PowerPoint 2007.

#	Objective
2.1.1	Insert and remove text boxes
2.1.2	Size text boxes
2.1.3	Format text boxes
	• Select fill
	• Select border
	• Select effects
2.1.4	Select text orientation and alignment
	• Set text direction
	• Set text alignment
2.1.5	Set margins
2.1.6	Create columns in text boxes
2.2.5	Create and format bulleted and numbered lists
	• Add bullets
3.3.4	Add text to shapes

Objects containing text

Explanation

Objects by themselves can enhance the overall message you want to convey in a presentation, but in some cases, adding descriptive text to objects makes your message much more effective.

Adding text to objects

When you add text to an object, the text becomes part of the object and moves along with it in a slide. However, if you resize the object, the text is not automatically resized.

To add text to an object, simply select the object and type the text. By default, the text is centered in the object. However, you can change the alignment of the text relative to the object.

Do it!

C-1:   Adding text to an object

Here's how	Here's why
1 Select the center star object	You'll add text to it.
2 Type **Morgan O.**	To add the text within the shape.
3 Observe the star	The text is centered within the star and is formatted with a white color.
4 Select the left star	
5 Type **Peyton J.**	
6 Select the right star and type **Michele C.**	
7 Update the presentation	

Modifying text in objects

Explanation

After you add text to objects, you can modify the text to improve the look of your presentation. To do so, select the text or the object containing the text, and use the options on the Mini toolbar or in the Font group (on the Home tab) to change the font, font size, and font color. You can also make the text bold, italic, underlined, or shadowed.

Do it!

C-2: Modifying text in an object

Here's how	Here's why
1 Point to the **Peyton J.** text	(In the left star.) The mouse pointer changes shape to an I-beam.
Click once	To place the insertion point in the text.
Press `CTRL` + `A`	To select all the text in the object.
2 Observe the selection	
	There is a white box around the text, indicating that it is selected.
3 Activate the Home tab	If necessary.
4 From the Font list, select **Arial Black**	(Located in the Font group.) To change the font.
From the Font Size list, select **20**	To increase the font size.
	Next, you'll format the text in the other two starts simultaneously.
5 Select the other two stars	Click the star containing Morgan O.; then press Ctrl and click the star containing Michele G.
Change the font to Arial Black and the font size to 20	When you do, the first names become too large for the objects.
6 Select all three stars	
7 Activate the Drawing Tools Format tab	
8 Using the Size group, change both the Height and Width to **2.8**	To enlarge the star objects to fit the text within them.
9 Press the arrow keys several times	(If necessary.) To nudge all three shapes to the left or right so they are again centered on the slide.
10 Update the presentation	

Drawing text boxes

Explanation

By default, when you select an object and type text, PowerPoint automatically creates a text box. You can also draw a text box on a slide and then enter text in it. As you add text to a text box, its width remains constant but the height adjusts to fit the text.

To create a text box and add text:

1 Click the Text Box button in either of these groups:
  - The Text group on the Insert tab.
  - The Insert Shapes group on the Drawing Tools Format tab.
2 Drag the mouse pointer to create a text box.
3 Type the text you want to add.
4 Resize and reposition the text box as you want.

To resize a text box, click the text box so that selection handles appear along the edges and on the corners. Drag a selection handle to resize the text box. If you want to delete a text box, point to an edge of the text box to select the text box, and press Delete.

Text formatting and orientation

You can format the text within a text box by using the same techniques you use to format other slide text. You can also specify the orientation for the text within a text box. For example, you can rotate the text 90 degrees or 270 degrees within the text box. To change the orientation of text within a text box:

1 Activate the Home tab.
2 In the Paragraph group, click the Text Direction button.
3 Choose a text direction.
4 Resize and move the text box as necessary.

C-3: Creating text boxes

Here's how	Here's why
1 Create a new blank slide	(On the Home tab, click the New Slide down arrow and select the Blank layout.) You'll add text listing new kiosk locations.
2 Activate the Insert tab	You'll create a text box displaying vertical text for the slide's title.
3 Click **Text Box**	(In the Text group.) You can now drag to create a text box.
4 Drag as shown	

5 Type **New kiosk locations**	
Format the text as Arial Black, 40 pt	You'll rotate the text 270 degrees.
6 Click	(The Text Direction button is in the Paragraph group.) To display the Text Direction list.
Choose **Rotate all text 270°**	The text is rotated, but appears jumbled within the text box. You'll resize the text box.
7 Point to the bottom-right text box handle	
	The pointer changes to a two-sided arrow.
Drag down and to the left, as shown	
	To resize the text box so that the text fits vertically on one line.

8 Point to an edge of the text box

Intersecting arrows appear at the tip of the pointer.

Drag to move the text box as shown

Text box formatting

Explanation

In addition to formatting the text within a text box, you can format the text box itself. You can format the text box fill and borders, and apply effects. To format a text box:

1　Select the text box. The Drawing Tools Format tab appears on the Ribbon.
2　Activate the Drawing Tools Format tab.
3　Apply formatting by using options in the Shape Styles group:
   - Click Shape Fill and choose a fill color.
   - Click Shape Outline and choose an outline color, weight, and style.
   - Click Shape Effects and choose an effect.

Text alignment and margins

You might want to change the alignment of text within a text box, or change the internal margin settings within the text box. You can do so by using options in the Home tab's Paragraph group:

- Click a horizontal alignment button to specify horizontal alignment.
- Click the Align Text button and choose Top, Middle, or Bottom to specify vertical alignment within the text box. You could also choose More Options to open the Format WordArt dialog box with the Text Box options showing, where you can specify additional alignment settings and internal margin settings.

Bullet formatting

By default, text you type in a text box does not appear bulleted. To apply bulleted list formatting, select the text and click the Bullets button to apply the default bullet style. To apply a specific bullet style, click the Bullets drop-down arrow and select a bullet style.

Text box columns

You can format a text box to display text in multiple columns. To do so:

1　Activate the Home tab.
2　Select the text box.
3　In the Paragraph group, click the Columns button and choose the number of columns you want the text box to use.

You can also click the Columns button and choose More Columns to open the Columns dialog box. In the Columns dialog box, specify a number of columns as well as a spacing value between columns, and then click OK.

Do it!   ## C-4: Formatting text boxes

Here's how	Here's why
1 Activate the Drawing Tools Format tab	The text box must be selected for this tab to appear.
2 Click **Shape Fill** and choose a light blue color	To apply the color to the text box fill.
3 Click **Shape Outline** and choose a dark blue color	To apply the color to the text box outline. You'll increase the outline weight.
4 Click **Shape Outline** and choose **Weight, 3 pt**	Next, you'll apply a bevel effect.
5 Click **Shape Effects**, point to **Bevel**, and click the Cool Slant bevel effect	You'll change the text box margin settings.
6 Activate the Home tab	
7 Click [Align Text button] and choose **More Options...**	(The Align Text button is in the Paragraph group.) To open the Format Text Effects dialog box.
8 Under Internal margin, change the Left and Right values to **0.2**	To add more space to the left and right of the text within the text box, which causes the text box width to increase.
9 Change the Top and Bottom values to **0.5**	
Click **Close**	The text might be forced to two lines. You'll change the text box height.
10 Set the text box height to 7.2 inches	Activate the Drawing Tools Format tab, and in the Size group, enter 7.2 in the Shape Height box.
11 Set the text box width to 1.1 inches	
12 Move the text box up	If necessary.

13 Create another text box as shown

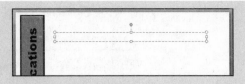

Activate the Insert tab, click Text Box, and drag to draw the text box.

14 Type **Dale** and press ⏎ ENTER

15 Enter the cities as shown

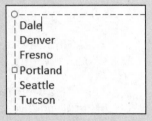

Dale
Denver
Fresno
Portland
Seattle
Tucson

16 Format the city names as Times New Roman, 44 pt

Select all the city names, and choose the formatting options from the Font group on the Home tab.

17 Click ☰ ▾

(The Bullets button is in the Paragraph group.) To apply bullet formatting to the selected items.

You'll display the city names in two columns.

18 Click ☰ ▾

(The Columns button is in the Paragraph group.) To display the Columns list.

Choose **Two Columns**

19 Resize the text box as shown

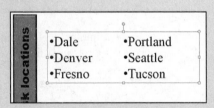

•Dale   •Portland
•Denver   •Seattle
•Fresno   •Tucson

(Point to the bottom center selection handle and drag up.) The text displays in two columns.

20 Update and close the presentation

Unit summary: Drawing objects

Topic A   In this topic, you used the drawing tools to **create basic shapes**.

Topic B   In this topic, you **applied formatting to selected objects**. Next, you **duplicated, deleted**, and **moved objects**. Then, you **modified objects** by resizing and rotating them. And finally, you **aligned multiple objects** to one another.

Topic C   In this topic, you **added text to an object**, **modified text in an object**, and **drew text boxes** on a slide.

Independent practice activity

In this activity, you'll draw an object, add text to it, apply formatting, and rotate it. Then, you'll create a text box, and position both the object and text box on the slide.

1 Create a new presentation. Change the slide layout for the first slide to Blank.

2 On the Home tab, in the Drawing group, display the Shapes gallery and click the Horizontal Scroll shape (located under Stars and Banners).

3 Drag to draw the shape across the slide.

4 Apply the shape style of your choice. Apply the fill color, outline color, and add effects of your choosing. (*Hint*: Use the Drawing Tools Format tab.)

5 Add the text **Employee of the Month** to the banner object. Apply the formatting of your choice to the text. Resize the banner object to display all the text on one line, if necessary.

6 Draw a text box at the bottom of the slide, add the text **Award**, and apply the formatting of your choice.

7 Use the Rotation handle to rotate the banner object slightly.

8 Align the banner object to the center of the slide. (*Hint*: On the Drawing Tools Format tab, click the Align button and choose **Align Center;** then click the Align button and choose **Align Middle**.)

9 Save the presentation as **My employee presentation** in the current unit folder.

10 Close the presentation.

Review questions

1 To draw a shape on a slide, you use which tab?

A Home

B Design

C Animations

D Slide Show

2 After an object is drawn, you change its shape by selecting it and performing what steps?

3 To change fill colors and outline colors and apply effects to a selected shape, you use the commands in which group?

A Insert Shapes

B Shape Styles

C Design

D Formatting

4 List the two methods you can use to duplicate an object (without using Copy and Paste).

5 To remove an object that is no longer needed, select it and _____.

6 When you select an object, the _____ handle and _____ handles appear around it.

7 List the steps you would perform to resize an object by dragging.

8 To rotate an object to a specific angle, select the object and then perform which of the following?

A In the Size group, place the insertion point in the Rotate box, enter the correct angle, and press Enter.

B In the Shape Styles gallery, select the angle you want.

C Click the Align button and choose Rotate. In the Rotate dialog box, enter the angle in the Rotation box and click Close.

D In the Size group, click the Dialog Box Launcher to open the Size and Position dialog box. Under Size and Rotate, enter the correct angle in the Rotation box and click Close.

9 What is the difference between a grid and a guide?

10 How do you add text to an object?

11 List the steps you use to draw a text box on a slide.

Unit 5

Graphics

Unit time: 45 minutes

Complete this unit, and you'll know how to:

A Create visually appealing text objects by using WordArt.

B Add images to a slide and modify the images by using options on the Picture Tools tab.

C Add clip art images to a slide by using the Clip Art task pane, and modify the clip art images.

Topic A: WordArt

This topic covers the following Microsoft Certified Application Specialist exam objectives for PowerPoint 2007.

#	Objective
2.2.2	Apply Quick Styles from the Style Gallery
2.2.7	Insert and modify WordArt • Create and format WordArt • Apply Quick Styles to WordArt • Change WordArt shape

WordArt effects

Explanation

You can use WordArt to create text that has special formatting applied to it. *WordArt* is a text object that has pre-designed effects that are applied when you create the object. Exhibit 5-1 shows a WordArt example that you can add to a slide.

Exhibit 5-1: An example of WordArt

Adding WordArt

To add a WordArt object:

1   Activate the Insert tab.
2   In the Text group, click WordArt to display the WordArt gallery.
3   Select a WordArt style to add a WordArt object in the center of the slide. The text is selected and ready for you to type.
4   Type to enter text in the WordArt object.

Editing WordArt

You edit the text in a WordArt object just as you would edit text in any other text placeholder. Click it to place the insertion point in the WordArt object, and then start editing. For example, you can type to add text, drag to select the desired text, or press Ctrl+A to select all the text.

Resizing and rotating WordArt

You can resize and rotate WordArt just as you would a graphic or other drawn object. To do so, select the object to display the rotate handle and sizing handles around it, and then perform one of the following:

- Drag a corner sizing handle to change the object's height and width, which causes the text to reflow within the object.
- Drag a sizing handle on the left or right side of the object to change only the width.
- Drag a sizing handle on the top or bottom of the object to change only the height.
- Drag the rotate handle to change the angle of the object.

Do it!

A-1: Adding and modifying WordArt

Here's how	Here's why
1 Create a new, blank presentation	
Save the presentation as **My new products**	In the current unit folder.
2 In the Title placeholder, enter **Outlander Spices**	
In the Subtitle placeholder, enter **New Product Line**	You are creating a presentation that will introduce Outlander Spices' new product line to the sales department.
3 Add a new slide with the Title Only slide layout	
4 In the Title placeholder, enter **Gourmet Collection**	This is the name of the new product line.
5 Activate the Insert tab	
Observe the Text group	It contains the WordArt button.

6 Click **WordArt**

To display the WordArt gallery.

Observe the WordArt gallery

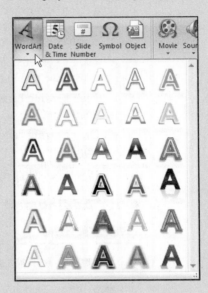

It contains a variety of WordArt styles.

7 Select the Fill – White, Outline – Accent 1 style, as shown

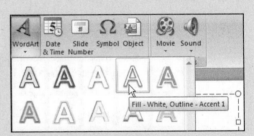

To insert a WordArt object on the center of the slide formatted with WordArt Style 1.

8 Observe the WordArt object

The placeholder text is selected and formatted with the desired style. As soon as you begin typing, the text will be replaced.

9 Type **Brand New**

To replace the placeholder text.

10 Verify that the insertion point is at the end of the line

As long as you haven't deselected the object, the insertion point should still be in place. If it isn't, click the text and use the arrow keys to place the insertion point at the end of the line.

11 Press (SPACEBAR)

To add a space.

Type **Next Month!**

To add more text to the WordArt object. The text object might extend off the slide's right edge.

12 Point to any edge of the WordArt
object

(Don't point to a handle.) The pointer appears as
an arrow pointing to intersecting arrows.

Drag to the left

To center the object on the slide.

13 Use the rotate handle to drag
counter-clockwise as shown

To rotate the object at a slight angle.

14 Deselect the object

15 Update the presentation

Formatting WordArt

Explanation

After you've created a WordArt object, you can edit it, change the WordArt style, and customize it with other formatting styles.

Selecting WordArt text

Before you apply a new WordArt style, it is important to note that selection matters. If you place the insertion point in the WordArt text and change the WordArt style, it will be applied only to part of the text, not necessarily all of it. Instead, you have to select all the text (drag to select or press Ctrl+A) or point to the edge of the WordArt object (the insertion point changes to a four-headed arrow) and click to select the entire object.

Using the WordArt Styles group

After the WordArt object is selected (or the text in the WordArt object is selected), the Drawing Tools Format tab appears. That is because WordArt objects are part of the new Office 2007 context sensitive feature.

In the WordArt Styles group, click Quick Styles to display a gallery of WordArt styles. Then, point to a style to see the live preview or select it to apply the style.

On the right of the WordArt Styles group, there are three buttons—Text Fill, Text Outline, and Text Effects. The following table describes them.

Name	Button	Description
Text Fill		Click the down arrow to the right of the button to display a gallery. You use this gallery to change the text fill color, remove the fill, or add a gradient or a texture.
Text Outline		Click the down arrow to the right of the button to display a gallery. You use this gallery to change the text outline color and other options.
Text Effects		Click the down arrow to the right of the button to display a menu. Each menu item displays a gallery that you can use to apply specific effects, such as Shadow, Reflection, Glow, Bevel, 3-D Rotation, and Transform.

Applying WordArt to text

Besides creating WordArt by using the WordArt button, you can also apply a WordArt style to existing text, such as the text in a Title placeholder. To format existing text by using WordArt styles, select the text and on the Drawing Tools Format tab, in the WordArt Styles group, click Quick Styles and select a style.

After the WordArt style is applied, you can change it or add other formatting by changing the font color or the outline color, or by applying additional effects.

Do it!

A-2:   Applying WordArt styles

Here's how	**Here's why**
1 In the WordArt object, place the insertion point in the word **Next**	You'll change the formatting by using the commands in the WordArt Styles group.
Activate the Drawing Tools Format tab	If necessary.
2 In the WordArt Styles group, click the More button	To display the gallery.
Under Applies to Selected Text, click the Fill – Accent 3, Outline – Text 2 style	(The last style in the top row.) To apply the style to the object.
3 Observe the WordArt object	
	Because you placed the insertion point in a single word instead of selecting all the text (Ctrl+A) or selecting the object (clicking on the edge of the object), the formatting was applied to only the one word.
4 Point to the edge of the WordArt object	The pointer changes to include a four-pointed arrow.
Click once	To select the WordArt object. You could also drag to select all the text in the object.
Apply the Fill – Accent 3, Outline – Text 2 style	All the text is formatted.
5 Display the Text Fill gallery	(In the WordArt Styles group, click the Text Fill button's down arrow.) You use this gallery to format the font fill.
Display the Text Outline gallery	(In the WordArt Styles group, click the Text Outline button's down arrow.) You use this gallery to specify the outline color and other outline formatting.
Display the Text Effects menu	(In the WordArt Styles group, click the Text Effects button.) Each submenu contains a gallery that you can use to apply specific effects.

6	In the Text Effects menu, point to **Glow**	You are going to add a glow effect to the WordArt object.
	Click the first glow variation	The Accent color 1, 5 pt glow variation.
7	Deselect the WordArt object	Next, you'll apply a WordArt style to existing text.
8	Select **Gourmet Collection**	(Triple-click the text in the Title placeholder.) The Drawing Tools Format group is still active. You'll apply a Word Art Style to this text.
9	Apply the WordArt style Fill – Text 2, Outline – Background 2	(The first style in the top row.) In the WordArt Styles group, click Quick Styles, and select the style.
10	Click the **Text Effects** button, and point to **Shadow**	To display the Shadow effects gallery.
	Select the Offset Diagonal Bottom Right effect	(The first shadow effect under Outer.) To apply a shadow to the "Gourmet Collection" text.
11	Click the Text Fill down arrow and select Olive Green, Accent 3	The Olive Green, Accent 3 swatch is a green color in the first row under Theme colors. It is the seventh swatch from the left.
12	Deselect the text	
13	Update the presentation	

Topic B: Pictures

This topic covers the following Microsoft Certified Application Specialist exam objectives for PowerPoint 2007.

#	Objective
3.3.1	Insert pictures from file
3.4.2	Add, change, and remove illustration effects
	• Remove background (transparencies)
	• Modify brightness and contrast
3.5.2	Order illustrations and other content
	• Bring to front and send to back
3.5.3	Group and align illustrations and other content

Pictures in presentations

Explanation

You can use images to convey ideas and information that can be difficult to express in words. With that in mind, it's a good idea to add images to a presentation whenever they will be useful. After you insert an image on a slide, you might be able to increase the visual appeal of that image by modifying it.

Inserting pictures

To insert a picture file:

1   Activate the Insert tab.
2   In the Illustrations group, click the Picture button to open the Insert Picture dialog box.
3   Navigate to the current unit and select the desired file.
4   Click Insert.

Using a slide layout to insert a picture

You can also use a slide layout to insert a picture. Here's how:

1   Insert a new slide with the Title and Content, Two Content, Comparison, Content with Caption, or Picture with Caption layout, or change the layout of an existing slide to one of those layout styles. Those layouts include an icon in the middle of the slide that you can click to insert a Picture, as well as icons for other content types.
2   On the icon in the middle of the slide, click the Picture button to open the Insert Picture dialog box.
3   Navigate to the current unit and select the desired file.
4   Click Insert.

Selecting a picture file

After you insert a picture file, it is selected automatically. A frame surrounds it, as shown in Exhibit 5-2, and sizing handles appear at each corner.

Exhibit 5-2: A selected picture file

Do it!

B-1: Inserting a picture

Here's how	Here's why
1 Activate the Insert tab	
2 In the Illustrations group, click **Picture**	To open the Insert Picture dialog box.
Navigate to the current unit folder	
Select **Gourmet Collection artwork**	This is a JPEG file provided by the art department. They are working on a new print ad campaign, and this artwork will be a major part of it.
3 Click **Insert**	To insert the picture file on the slide.
4 Observe the slide	The image is placed in the slide. The slide title is visible but the "Brand New Next Month!" WordArt object is under the picture.
5 Observe the picture	The picture is selected, and displays a rotate handle and sizing handles.
6 Observe the Ribbon	The Picture Tools Format tab is active. This is a context sensitive tab that appears when you select a placed picture file.
7 Update the presentation	

Working with pictures

Office 2007 offers many features that you can use to modify a picture file. All of these features are found on the Picture Tools Format tab, shown in Exhibit 5-3, which is part of the new Office 2007 context sensitive feature.

Exhibit 5-3: The Picture Tools Format tab

The following table describes some of the options available on the Picture Tools Format tab.

Button	Group	Description
Brightness	Adjust	Click to display the Brightness gallery, and select a style. The picture is either lightened or darkened.
Contrast	Adjust	Click to display the Contrast gallery, and select a style. The contrast of the picture will either increase or decrease.
Recolor	Adjust	Click to display the Recolor gallery, and select a style. A color effect is added to the selected picture. For example, you can select Set Transparent Color, and then click a color in a picture that should become transparent so that items behind the picture are visible through the now transparent area.
Compress Pictures	Adjust	Click to open the Compress Pictures dialog box. You use the features on this dialog box to reduce the picture and presentation file size.
Change Picture	Adjust	Click to open the Insert Picture dialog box to insert a new picture in place of the selected picture.
Reset Picture	Adjust	Click to remove the formatting applied to the selected picture, and return it to its original state.
Picture Shape	Picture Styles	Click to display the Picture Shape gallery, and select a shape within which the picture will display.
Picture Border	Picture Styles	Click to display the Picture Border gallery for applying a border to the selected picture. Select a border color, or format or remove the border.
Picture Effects	Picture Styles	Click to display the Picture Effects gallery, for adding effects to a picture, such as shadow, reflection, glow, soft edges, and 3-D rotation effects.

Button	Group	Description
Bring to Front	Arrange	Click the button to bring the selected object in front of all other objects on the slide. Click the down arrow and choose Bring Forward to bring the selected object forward one position in the stacking order.
Send to Back	Arrange	Click the button to send the selected object behind all other objects on the slide. Click the down arrow and choose Send Backward to send the selected object back one position in the stacking order.
Selection Pane	Arrange	Displays the Selection pane, which you can use to select objects, change their stacking order, or to hide or show objects.
Crop	Size	Click to activate the tool. The mouse pointer has the crop icon added to it. Point to the edge of a picture and drag to hide a portion of it.

The Picture Tools Format tab's Arrange group also includes Align, Group, and Rotate buttons, which each display a menu of options for working with pictures.

Do it!

B-2: Adjusting pictures

Here's how	Here's why
1 Verify that the picture is selected and the Picture Tools Format tab is active	
2 In the Adjust group, click **Brightness**	To display the Brightness gallery.
Point to each gallery option	To see the live preview applied to the picture.
Click **+10%**	To brighten the picture by 10%.
3 Click **Contrast**	To display the Contrast gallery.
Point to each gallery option	To see the live preview.
Click **-20%**	To reduce the contrast of the picture by 20%.
4 Click **Picture Effects** and point to **Shadow**	(In the Picture Styles group.) To display the Shadow gallery.
Click the Offset Right effect, as shown	
	To apply a shadow to the picture.
5 Click **Picture Effects** and point to **Soft Edges**	To display the Soft Edges gallery.
Click **5 Point**	To add a 5-point edge that fades to transparent along the picture's outer edge.
6 Deselect and observe the picture	You've added to the brightness, reduced the contrast, added a shadow, and applied a soft edge to the image.
	Next, you'll add a picture of mint leaves to the gourmet collection artwork image.
7 Insert the Mint image	Activate the Insert tab and click Picture. In the current unit folder, click Mint and click Insert.

8 Drag the mint image as shown

You'll set the white background to appear transparent so that only the mint leaves are visible.

9 In the Adjust group, click **Recolor** and choose **Set Transparent Color**

10 Point to the slide

The pointer changes to indicate that you can now click a color within the picture to set that color to transparent.

11 Point to the white area behind the mint leaves

Click the white area

To make it transparent. The image behind the mint leaves is now visible through the area that you set to transparent. However, a white fringe appears around the leaves. You'll adjust the brightness and contrast to reduce this effect.

12 Set the brightness to –10%

(Click Brightness and choose –10%.) To darken the picture.

13 Set the contrast to –40%

(Click Contrast and choose –40%.) The white fringe is less apparent.

14 Deselect the mint image

15 Update the presentation

Arranging and grouping items

Explanation

When a slide contains several items, you might need to arrange the items so that they overlap one another the way you want. In addition, you might want to group items so that you can select them as a single item.

Adjusting stacking order

By default, newer items you add to a slide appear in front of older items where they overlap. The order in which items overlap one another is called the *stacking order*. To modify the stacking order, select the item whose stacking order you want to change, and select an option from the Arrange group, which appears on several tabs. You can click the Bring to Front or Send to Back buttons to move an object, or you can click either button's down arrow to display a list with additional options for adjusting the stacking order.

Grouping items

If you position several items on a slide, and you want them to maintain their positions relative to one another, you can group them. In this way, you can select them as a single item and move them together. To group items, select them, click the Group button, and choose Group. You can ungroup selected items by clicking the Group button and choosing Ungroup.

Do it!

B-3: Arranging and grouping overlapping items

Here's how	Here's why
1 Select the WordArt object	You'll move this object in front of the other items.
Activate the Drawing Tools Format tab	If necessary.
2 In the Arrange group, click **Bring to Front**	(Not the down arrow.) To move the item in front of the other objects.
3 Click the edge of the WordArt object	To select the entire object.
Set the font size to **36**	
Move the WordArt object to the top-left corner of the picture, as shown	

(Point to an edge of the WordArt object's border and drag.) To position the WordArt object in relation to the picture.

4 Select the WordArt object and the two pictures	(With the WordArt object still selected, press Ctrl and click the main picture; then click the mint image.) The Drawing Tools Format and Picture Tools Format tabs are both available.
Activate the Picture Tools Format tab	You could also use the Drawing Tools Format tab.
5 In the Arrange group, click [⊞ ▾]	(The Group button.) To display the Group menu.
Choose **Group**	To combine the WordArt and picture objects into one selection. The picture frame has changed. Both the Drawing Tools Format and Picture Tools Format tabs are still available.
6 Click [⊞ ▾]	To display the Group menu.
Observe the menu	The only command available is Ungroup. You would select Ungroup to remove the grouping you just created.
7 Click [⊟ ▾]	(The Align button.) To display the Align menu.
Observe the Align menu	"Align to Slide" is checked, indicating that any alignment options you choose will align the selected object relative to the slide.
Choose **Align Center**	To align the picture to the horizontal center of the slide.
8 Click the **Align** button and choose **Align Middle**	To align the picture to the vertical center of the slide.
9 Update the presentation	

Topic C: Clip art

This topic covers the following Microsoft Certified Application Specialist exam objective for PowerPoint 2007.

#	Objective
3.3.3	Insert clip art

Clip art in presentations

Explanation

In addition to purchasing or creating your own image files to add to your presentations, you can add clip art objects. Some clip art objects are included with the Office Suite and PowerPoint, and are stored on your computer. Additional clip art objects are available on the Web.

Adding clip art

To add clip art to a slide:

1   Insert a new slide with the Title and Content, Two Content, Comparison, or Content with Caption layout, or change the layout of an existing slide to one of those layout styles. When you do, there are icons in the middle of the slide that you can use to insert a table, chart, clip art, picture, SmartArt graphic, or movie.

2   On the middle of the slide, click the Clip Art icon to open the Clip Art task pane.

3   On the Clip Art pane, display the Search in drop-down list and check the collections you want to search. Close the list.

4   In the Search for box, enter a description and click Go. The results of the search are displayed in the pane.

5   Insert the desired image on the slide by doing one of the following:

- Click an image.

- Drag an image onto the slide.

- Click the down arrow and choose Insert.

You also can insert a clip art object on any slide by activating the Insert tab and clicking the Clip Art button in the Illustrations group.

After inserting a clip art object, as shown in Exhibit 5-4, select it. Then, you can resize and format it as you would a picture file or a drawn shape.

Global Product Rollout

- Starts in North America next month
  - Specific date is TBD
  - Will coincide with new Web initiative
- Market plan
  - To be announced at Sales meeting
  - $250,000 budget
- Discussion
  - Customer concerns
  - Quality guarantee

Exhibit 5-4: A slide with a clip art object added

Do it!

C-1: Inserting and modifying clip art

Here's how	Here's why
1 Insert a new slide with the Title and Content layout	
In the Title placeholder, enter **Global Product Rollout**	
2 Observe the icons in the middle of the slide	
	There are six icons that you can use to add a table, chart, clip art, picture, SmartArt graphic, or Movie. You are going to use it to add a clip art object.
3 Click the **Clip Art** icon, as shown	
	(In the middle of the slide.) To display the Clip Art pane on the right side of the application window.
4 In the Clip Art pane, display the Search in drop down list	(Click the down arrow to the right of the list.) You can search for clip art in your own collections, the Microsoft Office collections on your computer, or collections on the Web.
Verify that My Collections and Office Collections are checked	
Clear **Web Collections**	If necessary.
Close the list	
5 In the Search for box, enter **globe**	You are looking for an image that goes with the "Global Product Rollout" slide.
Click **Go**	(Or press Enter.) To search the Clip Art collections on your computer. The search results are displayed in the Clip Art pane.

6 Point to the globe clip art image as shown

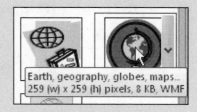

If you click the image, it will appear on the slide, and the content placeholder will be removed. To add the clip art image and keep the placeholder for adding text later, you'll drag the clip art onto the slide.

Click and hold the mouse button on the globe image, and drag it onto the slide

To add the clip art to the slide without deleting the content placeholder.

7 Click a blank area

To deselect all objects.

8 Double-click the globe clip art on the slide

To select it and activate the Picture Tools Format tab.

In the Size group, change the Height and Width to **2.25** inches

Select the number in the Height box, type "2.25" and press Enter to change both values.

9 Move the globe image to the bottom-right corner of the content placeholder

10 Place the insertion point in the content placeholder text

You'll finish the slide by adding text.

Enter the text shown

Global Product Rollout

- Starts in North America next month
  - Specific date is TBD
  - Will coincide with new Web initiative
- Market plan
  - To be announced at Sales meeting
  - $250,000 budget
- Discussion
  - Customer concerns
  - Quality guarantee

Press Enter and then press Tab to create a new sub-bullet. Then press Enter and press Shift+Tab to create a new main bullet.

11 Update the presentation

The Web Clip Art collection

Explanation

If the images available in the Office Suite and PowerPoint collections are not sufficient for your needs, you can access additional images from Microsoft's Web Collection.

To use the Web Collection:

1 Display the Clip Art pane.

2 Display the Search in drop-down list and check Web Collections. You can also clear My Collections and Office Collections to search only the online images.

3 In the Search for box, enter a description and click Go. PowerPoint connects to the Microsoft Web site and downloads the files that meet your search requirements. The results of the search are displayed in the pane.

4 Insert the desired image on the slide.

Another way to access Microsoft's online Clip Art collection is to display the Clip Art pane and click the "Clip art on Office Online" link at the bottom of the pane.

C-2: Inserting clip art from the Web Collections

Here's how	Here's why
1 Verify that the Clip Art pane is open	
2 In the Search in drop-down list, check **Web Collections**	You will search this collection of images.
Clear **My Collections** and **Office Collections**	You would probably normally leave these checked, but for the purpose of focusing on the Web Collection, you'll clear them.
3 Verify that globe is entered in the Search for box	You'll search the Web collections for a globe image that is better than the one you just inserted.
Click **Go**	
4 Observe the results	(Scroll through them.) To look at each image and identify an image that might be better.
5 Select the globe image on the slide	
Press (DELETE)	To remove it.
6 From the Clip Art results, drag a clip art image onto the slide	Select the image of your choice. Place the image in the bottom-right corner to replace the image you just deleted.
Adjust the size of the image	If necessary.
7 Close the Clip Art pane	
8 Update and close the presentation	

Unit summary: Graphics

Topic A   In this topic, you **added a WordArt object** to a slide. Then, you **modified a WordArt object** by applying different styles.

Topic B   In this topic, you **inserted images**. You also **adjusted and modified images** and **grouped items** together.

Topic C   In this topic, you **inserted a clip art object**. Next, you **modified the clip art** object. Finally, you inserted a clip art object from the **Web Collections**.

Independent practice activity

In this activity, you'll create and modify a WordArt object. Then, you'll add a slide, enter text, and insert a clip art image. Next, you'll add image files and modify them.

1 Create a new presentation, starting with a blank slide.

2 Create a WordArt text object with the text **Keys To Our Success** and the WordArt style of your choice.

3 Make the WordArt text bigger, and move it to the center of the slide. Modify the WordArt style with the formatting of your choice.

4 Insert a new slide with the Title and Content layout.

5 In the title placeholder, type **Keys To Our Success**.

6 Insert clip art of your choice without removing the content placeholder. (*Hint*: Drag the clip art from the Clip Art pane onto the slide.)

7 In the bulleted list, enter five bullets, as shown in Exhibit 5-5.

8 Save the presentation as **My success** in the current unit folder. Then close the presentation.

9 Open Practice images.

10 Save the presentation as **My practice images**.

11 On the second slide, insert the Cinnamon image from the current unit folder, and increase the brightness of the image.

12 On the third slide, insert the Mint image. Brighten the image.

13 On the fourth slide, insert the Nutmeg image. Modify the image with the options of your choice.

14 Update and close the presentation.

15 Close the Clip Art panel, if necessary.

Exhibit 5-5: The slide after step 7 of the Independent practice activity

Review questions

1 The WordArt button is located on which tab?

   A Home

   B Insert

   C Design

   D Animations

2 How do you edit WordArt text?

3 What is a quick and easy way to apply a new set of formatting to a WordArt object?

4 True or false? You can apply WordArt styles to existing text, such as a slide title.

5 List the steps necessary to display the Insert Picture dialog box?

6 How do you add a shadow to an imported picture?

7 True or false? After inserting a clip art image, you can't resize it but you can format it as you would a picture file or a drawn image.

8 True or false? You can use PowerPoint to search clip art collections stored on your computer, as well as collections on the Web.

Unit 6

Tables and charts

Unit time: 45 minutes

Complete this unit, and you'll know how to:

A Add a table to a presentation, enter text in the table, and format the table.

B Create and modify a chart by using the Insert Chart dialog box and the options on the Chart Tools tabs.

C Create and modify SmartArt objects by using the options on the SmartArt Tools tabs.

Topic A: Tables

This topic covers the following Microsoft Certified Application Specialist exam objectives for PowerPoint 2007.

#	Objective
3.7.1	Insert tables in a slide
3.7.2	Apply Quick Styles to tables
3.7.3	Change alignment and orientation of table text
3.7.4	Add images to tables

Tables in presentations

Explanation

You can add a table to any slide in your presentation. While working on a table, you can also modify it by inserting or deleting rows or columns.

Table structure

A table consists of rows and columns. The intersection of a row and a column is called a *cell*. You can add text or numbers to a cell. Exhibit 6-1 shows the structure of a table.

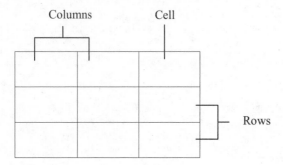

Exhibit 6-1: A sample table structure

Adding tables

There are several techniques you can use to add tables to your presentations. One way to add a table is to use one of the slide layouts that displays the Table icon, such as the Title and Content or the Two Content layouts. On the icon in the middle of the slide, click the Table icon to open the Insert Table dialog box. Enter the number of columns and rows you want, and click OK.

You can also add a table to any slide by using the Table button. To add a table by using the Table button:

1 Activate the Insert tab.

2 In the Tables group, click Table to display the Table menu.

3 In the Table menu, point to indicate the number of rows and columns you want in your table. As you do, you'll see a live preview of the table on the slide.

4 When the table is the size you want, click to add it to the slide.

Another way to add a table to any slide is by specifying values in the Insert Table dialog box. To add a table by using the Insert Table dialog box:

1 Activate the Insert tab.

2 In the Tables group, click Table to display the Table menu.

3 Choose Insert Table to open the Insert Table dialog box.

4 Specify the number of columns and rows you want.

5 Click OK.

A third way to create a table on any slide is by drawing the table. To draw a table:

1 Activate the Insert tab.

2 In the Tables group, click Table to display the Table menu.

3 Choose Draw Table.

4 Point to the slide and drag to draw the table. At first, the table includes a single cell.

5 Drag within the table to create rows and columns.

Table Tools tab

After you add a table to a slide, the Table Tools tabs appear. The two Table Tools tabs are the Design and Layout tabs, which you use to modify and format the table. Exhibit 6-2 shows the Table Tools Design tab.

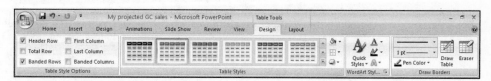

Exhibit 6-2: The Table Tools Design tab

Adding text to tables

You add text to a table the same way you add text to any other object. Text or numbers are entered in a table's cell. You move from one cell to another by pressing Tab, by using the arrow keys, or by clicking a cell.

When the insertion point is in the last cell of the last row and you press Tab, a new row is added to the table.

A-1: Adding a table

Here's how	Here's why
1 Open Projected GC sales	(From the current unit folder.) You'll insert a table into this presentation.
2 Save the presentation as **My projected GC sales**	
3 After slide 3, insert a new slide with the Title and Content layout	
4 In the title placeholder, enter **Projected Gourmet Collection Sales**	
5 In the content placeholder, click the table icon, as shown	
	To open the Insert Table dialog box.
Observe the Insert Table dialog box	
	You can specify the number of columns and rows in the table.
6 In the Number of columns box, enter **2**	You will insert a table that contains two columns and four rows.
In the Number of rows box, enter **4**	
Click **OK**	The table appears on the slide, and the Table Tools Design tab is activated.
7 Observe the Table Tools tabs	The Table Tools tabs appear on the Ribbon, because a table is selected.
Observe the Table Tools Design tab	It contains the Table Style Options, Table Styles, WordArt Styles, and Draw Borders groups.
Activate the Table Tools Layout tab	It contains the Table, Rows & Columns, Merge, Cell Size, Alignment, Table Size, and Arrange groups.
8 Type **2007**	To place the number in the first cell of the table.

9   Press (TAB)   To move to the next cell in the table.

    Observe the cell   The insertion point appears in the cell,
                                       indicating that you can add text to it.

10 Type **Overall Projected
    Sales**

    Press (TAB)   To select the first cell in the second row.

11 Type **1st Quarter**

12 Complete the table as shown

2007	Overall Projected Sales
1st Quarter	$100,000
2nd Quarter	$120,000
3rd Quarter	$150,000

13 Press (TAB)   To add a new row and select the first cell in the
                                       new row.

14 Type **4th Quarter** and move to
    the next cell

    Type **$175,000**

15 Update the presentation

Modifying tables

Explanation

While working on a table, you might have to increase or decrease the size and width of an existing row or column to fit the content. You do this by dragging the column or row boundaries. If you need to insert a new row or column, use the buttons in the Rows & Columns group, shown in Exhibit 6-3.

Exhibit 6-3: The Table Tools Layout tab

The following table lists techniques for adding rows and columns by using the buttons in the Rows & Columns group.

Button Name	Description
Insert Above	Select a cell; then click Insert Above to insert a new row above the current row.
Insert Below	Select a cell; then click Insert Below to insert a new row below the current row.
Insert Left	Select a cell; then click Insert Left to insert a new column to the left of the current column.
Insert Right	Select a cell; then click Insert Right to insert a new column to the right of the current column.

To delete a row or a column, select the row or column that you want to delete. In the Rows & Columns group, click Delete to display a menu. Choose Delete Columns to remove the column containing the selected cell, or choose Delete Rows to remove the row.

Do it!

A-2:   Modifying a table

Here's how	Here's why
1 Observe the table	Both columns are wider than necessary.
2 Point to the line separating the two columns, as shown	The pointer's shape changes to indicate that you can now drag to adjust the column width.

3 Drag the column boundary to the
   left, as shown

2007	Overall Projected Sales
1st Quarter	+‖+$100,000
2nd Quarter	$120,000
3rd Quarter	$150,000
4th Quarter	$175,000

The width of the second column increases, and
the text in the first column fits better.

Next, you'll increase the height of the top row.

4 Point to the bottom of the first
   row, as shown

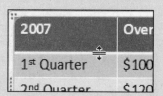

The pointer's shape changes to indicate that you
can now drag to adjust the row height.

   Drag down slightly, as shown

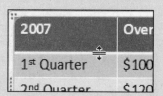

To increase the height of the first row.

5 Point just inside the right edge of
   the table, as shown

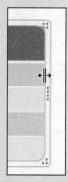

You'll resize the right column without resizing
the left column. To resize the table so that both
columns resize, you would drag from the right
resize handle.

6 Drag to the left as shown

2007	Overall Projected Sales
1st Quarter	$100,000
2nd Quarter	$120,000
3rd Quarter	$150,000
4th Quarter	$175,000

To reduce the size of the second column and the entire table.

7 Verify that the insertion point is still within the last cell

You'll add a row above the last row.

Verify that the Table Tools Layout tab is active

8 In the Rows & Columns group, click **Insert Above**

To insert a row above the current row. You won't need the new row, so you'll delete it.

Click **Delete** and choose **Delete Rows**

(In the Rows & Columns group.) To remove the row you just inserted. The first cell in the last row is now selected.

9 Click **Insert Left**

To insert a column to the left of the current column.

Click **Delete** and choose **Delete Columns**

To remove the column you just inserted.

10 Place the insertion point in the last cell

Click **Insert Below**

(Or press Tab.) To add a row at the bottom of the table.

11 Resize the table columns to fit the text

The text should fit on one line within each cell.

12 Add the text in the last row as shown

2007	Overall Projected Sales
1st Quarter	$100,000
2nd Quarter	$120,000
3rd Quarter	$150,000
4th Quarter	$175,000
TOTAL	$545,000

13 Update the presentation

Formatting tables

Explanation

Before applying styles and other formatting, you have to be sure that the part of the table you want to format is selected. The following table describes three common selection techniques that you will use with tables.

Pointer shape	Description
	Point to the edge of the table and the mouse pointer changes to a four-headed arrow. Click to select the entire table.
	Just outside the table (on either the left or right side), point to a row and the pointer changes to a black arrow. Click to select the row, or click and drag to select multiple rows.
	Just outside the table (on either the top or bottom), point to a column and the pointer changes to a black arrow. Click to select the column, or click and drag to select multiple columns.

Aligning text in a cell

You can change the horizontal and vertical alignment of text within a cell. To do that, select the desired cell(s), row(s) or columns(s). Activate the Table Tools Layout tab, and in the Alignment group, click the appropriate button. The following table describes them.

Button Name	Description
Align Left	Aligns the selected text to the left side of its cell.
Align Right	Aligns the selected text to the right side of its cell.
Center	Aligns the selected text between the left and right edge of its cell.
Align Top	Aligns the selected text to the top of its cell.
Center Vertically	Aligns the selected text between the top and bottom edge of its cell.
Align Bottom	Aligns the selected text to the bottom of its cell.

In addition to changing the text alignment, you can use options in the Alignment group to change text orientation. To change text orientation in a cell, in the Alignment group, click Text Direction and choose an option. For example, you can specify that the text in a cell be rotated 90 degrees.

Table Tools Design tab

Most formatting changes you will make to a selected table require you to use the Table Tools Design tab. It contains several groups.

In the Table Style Options group, check the desired options and clear the ones you don't want. You will immediately see the changes applied to the selected table.

In the Table Styles group, point to a quick style to see its live preview and click to apply it. You can also use the Shading, Borders, and Table Effects buttons to change colors and add more interesting formatting.

Do it!

A-3: Formatting a table

Here's how	Here's why
1 Point to the top of the right column, as shown	
Click once	To select the column.
2 Activate the Table Tools Layout tab	If necessary.
3 Click	(The Center button is in the Alignment group.) To center the text in the column.
4 Point as shown	
Click once	To select the row.
5 Click	(The Center Vertically button is in the Alignment group.) To center the text between the top and bottom edges of the row.
6 Activate the Table Tools Design tab	
7 In the Table Style Options group, clear **Header Row**	To change the way the top row is formatted.
Experiment with the options	(In the Table Style Options group.) Check and clear each option to see the effect.
Set the options as shown	
8 In the Table Styles group, click any style	To specify the table style of your choice.

9 Click   (The Effects button is in the Table Styles group.)
                                           To display the Table Effects menu.

   Point to **Shadow**   To display the Shadow gallery.

   Select Offset Diagonal Bottom
   Right, as shown

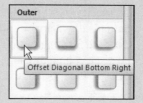

                                           To apply a shadow effect to the table.

10 Click the edge of the table, as
    shown

                                           To select the table.

    Move the table to the slide's   It doesn't have to be exact.
    center

11 Deselect the table   To view the finished table.

12 Update the presentation

Cell fill options

Explanation

You can fill table cells with a solid color, picture, gradient, or texture. A cell fill applies to the cell background behind any text within the cell. You can add cell fills by using the Shading list on the Table Tools Design tab.

To specify a cell fill, select the cell or cells you want to fill; then click the Shading button's down arrow and select a fill type. For example, to add an image to a table cell, click the Shading button's down arrow and choose Picture. In the Insert Picture dialog box, select a picture and click Insert. The picture fits to the cell's dimensions, and you can still type to add text within the cell with the image in the cell background.

Do it!   **A-4:   Adding images to a table**

Here's how	Here's why
1 Open Spice pricing	In the current unit folder.
2 Save the presentation as **My spice pricing**	
3 Go to slide 2	You'll add images to the cells in the first column.
4 Click in the cell below Spice image	Next to "Cinnamon."
5 Activate the Table Tools Design tab	
6 Click the Shading down arrow	

In the Table Styles group.

Choose **Picture...**	To open the Insert Picture dialog box.
7 Select **Cinnamon**	In the current unit folder.
Click **Insert**	
8 Press ⬇	To move the insertion point to the cell below the cinnamon image.
9 Insert the Mint image	Click the Shading down arrow and choose Picture. Select Mint and click Insert.
10 In the cell below, insert the Nutmeg image	

11 Update and close the presentation

Topic B: Charts

This topic covers the following Microsoft Certified Application Specialist exam objectives for PowerPoint 2007.

#	Objective
3.6.1	Insert charts
3.6.2	Change chart types
3.6.3	Format fill and other effects
3.6.4	Add chart elements
	• Legend
	• Title

Charts in a presentation

Explanation

Charts are the graphical representations of numeric data. PowerPoint includes several chart types for you to choose from and includes multiple formatting options that you can use to modify them.

Inserting a chart

There are two methods you can use to create a chart. You can create a chart by clicking the Chart icon on a content slide layout, or by activating the Insert tab and clicking the Chart button in the Illustrations group. Both methods will open the Insert Chart dialog box. In this dialog box, select a chart type in the left pane. In the right pane, select the specific chart you want to create, and click OK. The chart is placed on the slide and Microsoft Excel 2007 opens.

The sample numerical data is contained in the Excel worksheet and the corresponding chart is displayed in the PowerPoint slide. Edit the data in Excel to customize the chart, and close Excel when you are done.

Do it!

B-1: Creating a chart

Here's how	Here's why
1 Insert a new slide with a Title and Content layout	In the My projected GC sales presentation.
2 In the title placeholder, type **Comparison Chart**	
3 Click the Chart icon, as shown	
	To open the Insert Chart dialog box.

4 In the left pane, select **Pie**	To view the available Pie charts.
Select the second pie chart, as shown	
Click **OK**	Microsoft Excel 2007 starts, and appears alongside the PowerPoint window.
5 In Excel, click as shown	
	To select the cell.
Type **Projected sales**	To add a heading.
Press (↵ ENTER)	To select the cell below.
6 Type **$100**	This represents the $100,000 that the Gourmet Collections brand is projected to sell in the first quarter.
Press (↵ ENTER)	To select the next cell below.
7 Type **$120**	To specify the value projected for the second quarter sales.
Press (↵ ENTER)	
Type **$150**	
Press (↵ ENTER)	
Type **$175**	
8 Click as shown	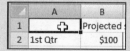
	(To select the cell.) You want to make sure you don't select a cell other than one of the cells that has text or numbers in it.
9 Observe the chart	(In the PowerPoint window.) The pie chart has four slices and a legend to the right identifying what each color represents.
10 Close Excel	(Click the Close button.) You're returned to PowerPoint; its window maximizes.
11 Update the presentation	

Change chart type

Explanation

If you want to change the chart type for an existing chart, then activate the Chart Tools Design tab, and in the Type group, click Change Chart Type. In the Change Chart Type dialog box that appears, specify a new chart type and click OK.

Do it!

B-2:   Changing the chart type

Here's how	Here's why
1 Activate the Chart Tools Design tab	(If necessary.) You'll change the chart type.
2 In the Type group, click **Change Chart Type**	To open the Change Chart Type dialog box.
3 Under Pie, click as shown	 To select the Exploded pie in 3-D chart type.
4 Click **OK**	 You'll decrease the space between the slices.
5 Point to the bottom slice Press and hold the mouse button and drag up	You can drag a slice toward the center to decrease the space between slices. To decrease the space between slices. If a single slice is selected, only that slice will move. To select all slices when dragging, click outside the slices but within the chart bounding box to deselect all slices; then begin dragging a slice.

Formatting charts

Explanation

After your data has been entered, you will most likely want to begin modifying the chart. To modify a chart, you can change the chart formatting and apply styles. You can alter the graphical representation of your data so that it's easier for your audience to comprehend.

You can format each individual chart element, or you can format the entire chart. The commands for formatting charts are found on the Chart Tools tabs, which are the Design, Layout, and Format tabs.

The Chart Tools Format tab

The Chart Tools Format tab contains five groups. The Current Selection group contains three options. You use the Chart Elements list to select specific parts of the chart. Or, you can click a chart element and look at this list to identify the selected element. After you've selected a chart element, click the Format Selection button to open the Format dialog box and make the necessary changes to the chart element.

As with other style groups, you use the Shape Styles group to apply styles, change a shape fill or outline, and apply an effect.

Chart Tools Layout tab

The Chart Tools Layout tab contains six groups. Use the Insert group to add a shape, a text box, or a picture to the chart. You can use the other groups to add, remove, and edit the elements of a chart.

Chart legend

When you create a chart, it typically displays a legend by default. However, you can hide or show a legend, and you can change the legend position. To add, remove, or position the chart legend, activate the Chart Tools Layout tab, and in the Labels group, click Legend and choose an option.

Chart labels

You also can add, remove, or position the chart title, along with other chart labels, by using the other options in the Labels group in the Chart Tools Layout tab. For example, to add, remove, or reposition a chart's title, activate the Chart Tools Layout tab, and in the Labels group, click Chart Title and choose an option.

Do it!

B-3: Formatting a chart

Here's how	Here's why
1 Observe the Chart Tools tabs	Chart Tools — Design Layout Format
	There are three Chart Tools tabs—Design, Layout, and Format. The Chart Tools Design tab is activated by default.
2 In the Chart Styles group, click the More down arrow	To display the gallery of available layouts.
Click **Style 32**	

3 On the slide, click the Chart Title text	To select the placeholder.
Click the Chart Title text again	
	To place the insertion point in the placeholder.
Edit the text to read **Projected Sales for Gourmet Collections**	
4 Click the edge of the chart frame	To deselect the chart title.
5 Activate the Chart Tools Layout tab	You'll hide the legend.
6 Click **Legend**	(In the Labels group.) To display the Legend list.
Choose **None**	To remove the legend.
	You'll add the legend, but at a different location.
7 Click **Legend** and choose **Show Legend at Left**	To add the Legend to the left of the chart.
	Next, you'll remove the chart title.
8 Click **Chart Title** and choose **None**	(In the Labels group.) To remove the chart title.
	You'll add the title back to the chart.
9 Click **Chart Title** and choose **Above Chart**	The chart title returns, but appears as the original title, rather than the version you edited.
	Next, you'll format an individual pie slice.
10 Click the top-left slice	All slices are selected.
Click the same slice again	To select that slice individually.
11 Activate the Chart Tools Format tab	
12 Click Shape Fill and select the Red, Accent 2 color	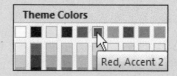
	To change the slice to red.
13 Update the presentation	

Topic C: Diagrams

This topic covers the following Microsoft Certified Application Specialist exam objectives for PowerPoint 2007.

#	Objective
3.1.1	Create a SmartArt diagram
	• Hierarchy
3.2.1	Add text to SmartArt diagrams
3.2.2	Change theme colors
3.2.3	Add effects using Quick Styles
3.2.4	Change the layout of diagrams
3.2.5	Change the orientation of charts
3.2.6	Add or remove shapes within SmartArt

Diagrams in PowerPoint

Explanation

You can use PowerPoint to create diagrams, such as organization charts, that visually represent relationships or processes.

Diagram types

You can insert a diagram by using the Choose a SmartArt Graphic dialog box, shown in Exhibit 6-4. You can choose from some of the commonly used standard diagrams, such as organization charts, cycle diagrams, or Venn diagrams.

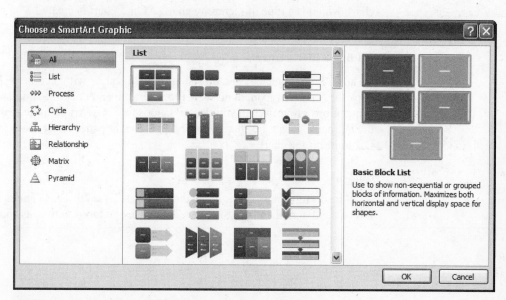

Exhibit 6-4: The Choose a SmartArt Graphic dialog box

The Choose a SmartArt Graphic dialog box divides the diagrams into seven categories, which are described in the following table.

Diagram	Description
List	Shows non-sequential blocks of information, grouped blocks of information, or sequential steps in a task, process, or workflow. For example, use this diagram to show three sales teams that each contain several employees.
Process	Shows steps leading toward a goal. For example, use this diagram to show the steps involved in hiring a new employee.
Cycle	Shows the steps of a cyclical process. For example, use this diagram to describe the process of developing a product, marketing it, and reinvesting profit in further development.
Hierarchy	Shows the hierarchical relationships among elements. For example, use an organization chart to represent the positions in an organization.
Relationship	Shows the relationship among items. For example, use a Venn diagram to show company resources used by two departments, differentiating among shared resources and resources used only in a given department.
Matrix	Shows the relationship of components to a whole in quadrants. For example, use this diagram to display the names of four departments within a division.
Pyramid	Shows containment, foundation-based, hierarchical, interconnected, overlapping, or proportional relationships. For example, use this diagram to display the food groups ordered from those you should eat often to those you should eat sparingly.

Creating a hierarchy chart

You can display the hierarchical details of your company by using an organization chart, which is a type of hierarchy chart. After a chart is created, you can add different levels to it, edit it, and change the formatting.

Adding a hierarchy chart

To add a hierarchy chart to a presentation, add a slide with a content slide layout and click the SmartArt icon, or activate the Insert tab and click the SmartArt button in the Illustrations group. When you do, the Choose a SmartArt Graphic dialog box opens. In the left pane, select the chart type, and in the right pane, select a specific chart. Click OK to insert the chart.

SmartArt Tools tabs

After inserting a new diagram, the diagram is selected, a Text Pane is displayed to the left of the diagram and the SmartArt Tools Design tab is active, as shown in Exhibit 6-5.

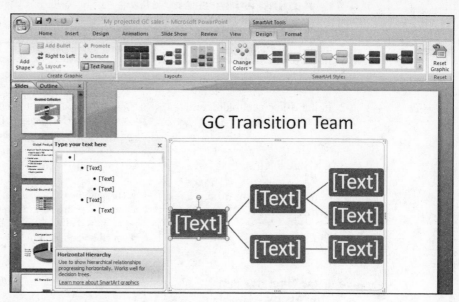

Exhibit 6-5: A hierarchy chart added to a slide

Adding text to a diagram

To use the Text Pane to add text, click the top bullet item to place the insertion point in that line, and then type to add the text. Click the next bullet item and type to complete that one. Repeat until all the chart boxes are full. The indent level of each item in the Text Pane corresponds to each item's position in the chart. The further an item is indented in the Text Pane, the lower it appears in the chart's hierarchy.

To add another box below a specific box by using the Text Pane:

1 In the Text Pane, place the insertion point to the right of the text corresponding to the box below which you want to add a new item and press Enter to add another box at the same level.

2 Press Tab to demote the item down so its box appears below the initial box in the chart.

3 Type to insert the text in the new box.

You can promote an existing item by clicking the item's name in the Text Pane and pressing Shift+Tab. To demote an item, place the insertion point in the item's name and press Tab.

If you don't want to use the Text Pane, you can close it by clicking the Text Pane button located on the SmartArt Tools Design tab, in the Create Graphics group. You can then select a chart box and type to add text. In addition, you can use the Create Graphic group's options to add, promote, and demote items.

Do it!

C-1: Adding a hierarchy chart

Here's how	Here's why
1 Insert a new slide with the Title Only layout	
2 In the title placeholder, enter **GC Transition Team**	You'll be adding a small hierarchy chart that shows who is in charge of what while getting the Gourmet Collections brand of spices started up.
3 Activate the Insert tab	If necessary.
In the Illustrations group, click **SmartArt**	To open the Choose a SmartArt Graphic dialog box. There are several types of SmartArt graphics that you can create. On this slide, you'll be adding a hierarchy (or an organization chart).
4 In the left pane, select **Hierarchy**	To display the various hierarchy options.
Select the **Horizontal Hierarchy** diagram type	
Click **OK**	
5 Observe the SmartArt object	(As shown in Exhibit 6-5.) The SmartArt Tools tabs appear—Design and Format. To the left of the object is a Text Pane you can use to add text to the chart.
6 In the Text Pane, verify that the insertion point appears next to the first item	Type your text here ✕ • [Text] • [Text] • [Text] • [Text] The text you enter here will be added to the first box in the hierarchy.
7 Enter **Kathy Sinclair, President**	Kathy will head up this project.

8 Click the next bullet

    To place the insertion point in it.

Add the text as shown

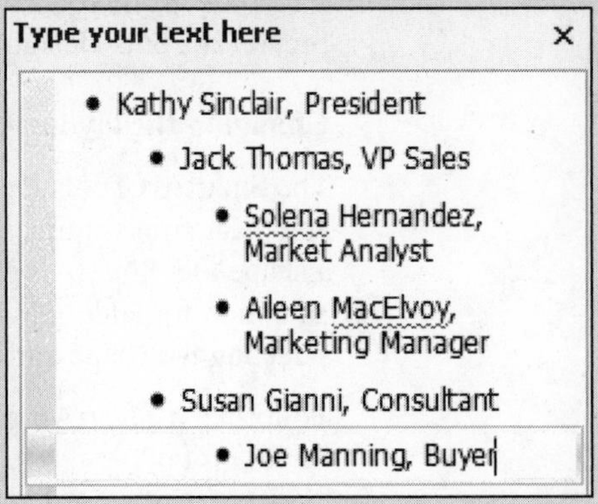

Type your text here	✕
• Kathy Sinclair, President	
• Jack Thomas, VP Sales	
• Solena Hernandez, Market Analyst	
• Aileen MacElvoy, Marketing Manager	
• Susan Gianni, Consultant	
• Joe Manning, Buyer	

9 In the Create Graphic group, click **Text Pane**

    To hide the Text Pane.

Observe the slide

    The hierarchy object is added and each box has text in it.

10 Update the presentation

Modifying diagrams

Explanation

After you've inserted a diagram and added text to it, you can modify it by using the SmartArt Tools Design and Format tabs.

Changing the layout

The SmartArt Tools Design tab has the tools you need to quickly change the layout of an object, apply quick styles, add shapes, and move shapes around. For example, to add a shape to a SmartArt graphic, in the Create Graphic group, click Add Shape and select an option for adding a new shape. You can remove a shape from a SmartArt graphic by selecting the shape and pressing Delete.

To format a SmartArt object by applying a quick style, select a style from the SmartArt Styles group.

You can change a graphic's theme colors by selecting from the Change Colors list in the SmartArt Styles group. You also can change the graphic's colors and apply effects by selecting from the SmartArt Styles group.

Formatting the object

The SmartArt Tools Format tab has five groups on it—Shapes, Shape Styles, WordArt Styles, Arrange, and Size. To use these options, select a box or multiple boxes in the chart. Then, in the Shapes group, you can change the shape and increase or decrease the size. In the WordArt Styles group, you can change the text colors and text outline formatting. To use the WordArt styles, select text in a box and then apply the desired style.

Flipping SmartArt graphics

You can flip a SmartArt graphic to reverse its orientation. To flip a graphic, activate the SmartArt Tools Design tab, and in the Create Graphics group, click Right to Left. Click the same button again to return the graphic to its original orientation.

Do it!

C-2: Modifying a hierarchy chart

Here's how	Here's why
1 Activate the SmartArt Tools Format tab	You'll increase the size of each box, apply a new style, and modify the formatting.
2 Select all six boxes in the hierarchy	Click an edge of the first box, press Ctrl, and click any part of a second box. Press Ctrl and click the remaining boxes.
3 In the Shapes group, click **Larger** twice	To increase the size of each box.
4 Activate the SmartArt Tools Design tab	
5 In the Layouts group, click the More down arrow	To display the Layouts gallery.
Click the **Organization Chart** layout	To apply a new layout to the hierarchy object.

6	Drag the bottom sizing handle down	(The middle sizing handle, not a corner.) To increase the size of the chart.
7	Select the **Joe Manning** box	(Click the edge of the box.) Joe Manning reports directly to Kathy Sinclair, so you need to reposition his box.
	In the Create Graphic group, click **Promote**	To move the box up one level. It is now even with Susan Gianni, indicating that Joe Manning reports directly to Kathy Sinclair.
8	Deselect the box and select the entire object	Click the edge of the object frame.
	In the SmartArt Styles group, display the gallery of available styles	Click the More down arrow.
	Under 3D, click the **Polished** style	To change the style.
9	In the SmartArt Styles group, click **Change Colors**	To display the Change Colors gallery.
	Under Colorful, click the **Colorful – Accent Colors** theme	
10	Select the **Joe Manning** box	You'll add a box under it.
	In the Create Graphic group, click the **Add Shape** down arrow	
	Click **Add Shape Below**	To add a position that reports to Joe Manning.
11	Type **Matt Smith, Assistant Buyer**	To add the name and title to the box.
		Finally, you'll flip the chart.
12	In the Create Graphic group, click **Right to Left**	To flip the chart.
13	Deselect the object	
	Update and close the presentation	

Unit summary: Tables and charts

Topic A   In this topic, you **added a table** to a slide. Next, you **modified** and **formatted the table**.

Topic B   In this topic, you **created a chart** on a slide. Then, you **modified the chart** by changing its formatting.

Topic C   In this topic, you **added a SmartArt hierarchy chart** to a slide. Next, you **modified the hierarchy chart** by formatting it and adding additional boxes.

Independent practice activity

In this activity, you'll create a table, add text, modify it, and apply formatting. Then, you'll create a hierarchy chart, add text, and apply formatting to it.

1 Create a new, blank presentation with a Title and Content layout slide.

2 Type **Sales (in Dollars)** in the title placeholder.

3 Add a 6-column, 5-row table to the slide.

4 Complete the table, as shown in Exhibit 6-6.

5 Delete the last row and last column.

6 Resize the table and move it to the center of the slide. Apply the formatting of your choice and compare the table to the one shown in Exhibit 6-7.

7 Add another slide that uses the Title and Content layout.

8 Type **The Project Team** in the title placeholder.

9 Insert a SmartArt hierarchy chart and add the text shown in Exhibit 6-8 to the hierarchy chart. (*Hint*: Press Tab to indent an item, or press Shift+Tab to remove an indent.)

10 Apply the formatting of your choice and compare your chart to the one shown in Exhibit 6-9.

11 Save the presentation as **My sales** and close it.

Sales (in Dollars)

	1st Qtr	2nd Qtr	3rd Qtr	4th Qtr	
Cumin	30	45	45	30	
Thyme	50	80	80	60	
Oregano	85	60	60	75	

Exhibit 6-6: The Sales table data for step 4 of the Independent practice activity

Sales (in Dollars)

	1st Qtr	2nd Qtr	3rd Qtr	4th Qtr
Cumin	30	45	45	30
Thyme	50	80	80	60
Oregano	85	60	60	75

Exhibit 6-7: The Sales table after step 6 of the Independent practice activity

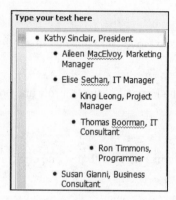

Exhibit 6-8: The chart text for step 9 of the Independent practice activity

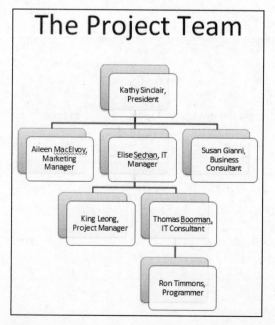

Exhibit 6-9: The organization chart after step 10 of the Independent practice activity

Review questions

1 What is a table cell?

2 How many ways are there to add a table to a slide?

   A One

   B Two

   C Three

   D More than three

3 True or false? After a table is added to a slide, the Table Tools tabs appear.

4 What keyboard keys do you use to move from one cell to another in a table?

5 When the insertion point is in the last cell of the last row and you press Tab, what happens?

6 How do you select an entire row in a table with just one click?

7 What is a chart used for?

8 You've just begun creating a chart by clicking the Chart button in the Illustration group. What step would you perform next?

9 Which tabs contain the groups and tools you use to modify and format a SmartArt object?

Unit 7

Modifying presentations

Unit time: 75 minutes

Complete this unit, and you'll know how to:

A Modify a presentation by using a template.

B Make global changes to a presentation by using the Master Slide view.

C Add visual appeal to the slide show by using transitions and timings.

D Prepare for a slide show by adding speaker notes.

E Set up a slide show for a speaker and a kiosk.

Topic A: Templates and themes

This topic covers the following Microsoft Certified Application Specialist exam objective for PowerPoint 2007.

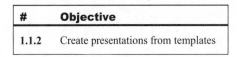

#	Objective
1.1.2	Create presentations from templates

Templates

Explanation

You can change the appearance of a presentation by applying a template to it. Templates contain themes, slide masters, and title masters that provide a consistent format and look for a presentation. After you apply a template, each slide you add to the presentation will have the same customized look. PowerPoint comes with a wide variety of professionally designed templates and even more available from Microsoft Office Online.

Using templates

To create a new presentation based on a template:

1 Click the Office button and choose New to open the New Presentation dialog box, shown in Exhibit 7-1.

2 In the left pane, select Installed Templates to access the templates stored on your computer, or select one of the options under Microsoft Office Online to access the templates available for download from Microsoft's Web site. After you select a template category, the templates are displayed in the right pane.

3 Select a design template.

4 Click Create.

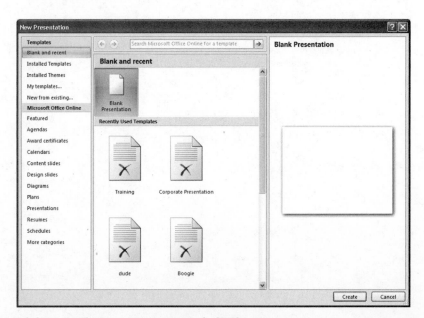

Exhibit 7-1: The New Presentation dialog box

Do it!

A-1: Creating a presentation based on a template

Here's how	Here's why
1 Open the New Presentation dialog box	Click the Office button and choose New.
2 In the left pane, under Microsoft Office Online, click **Presentations**	To view the presentation templates available at Microsoft Office Online. If you don't have an Internet connection, skip this step.
3 Under Templates, click **Installed Templates**	(In the left pane.) To view the templates installed on your computer.
4 In the right pane, select **Introducing PowerPoint 2007**	You'll use this template to create a new presentation.
Click **Create**	To create the presentation.
5 Set the slide to fit to the window	(In the status bar, click the Fit slide to current window button.)
	The template generates multiple sample slides. You'll delete all the sample slides.
6 Delete all slides	In the status bar, click the Slide Sorter button, select all slides, and press Delete.
7 Return to Normal view	In the status bar, click the Normal button.
8 Click the screen	To add the first slide.
9 Type **Outlander Spices** as the title of the slide	
10 Insert a new slide	(Click the New Slide button.) The new slide has the same design template applied to it.
11 Save the presentation as **My presentation**	In the current unit folder.
Close the presentation	

Using themes

Explanation

When you create a presentation based on a template, you give your slides a professional look and feel. Another way to quickly apply a professional appearance to your slides is by applying themes.

To apply a theme to an existing presentation:

1 Activate the Design tab.

2 In the Themes group, shown in Exhibit 7-2, point to a theme to see the live preview applied to the selected slide. Click the More down arrow to display the Themes gallery and point to a theme to see the live preview.

3 Click a theme to apply it.

Exhibit 7-2: The Themes group

Using multiple themes in a single presentation

You can apply a theme to the entire presentation or to specific slides. You can apply multiple themes within a single presentation. To apply multiple design themes in a single presentation:

1 In Slide Sorter view or Normal view, select the slides to which you want to apply a different design theme.

2 Activate the Design tab.

3 In the Themes group, right-click the desired theme and choose Apply to Selected Slides.

Do it!

A-2: Changing the design themes

Here's how	Here's why
1 Open GC announcement meeting	From the current unit folder.
2 Save the presentation as **My GC announcement meeting**	
3 Activate the Design tab	
4 In the Themes group, click the More down arrow	To display the Themes gallery.
In the Themes gallery, click the **Solstice** theme	(The themes are in alphabetical order.) To apply the Solstice theme to the presentation.
5 Go to slide 2 and observe the title	The title on this slide was previously formatted individually, and it still displays that custom formatting. You'll set this slide to use only the formatting specified by the current theme.
6 Activate the Home tab	
In the Slides group, click **Reset**	To apply the current Theme's formatting to the entire slide, removing the custom formatting that had been applied to the title.
7 Observe each slide in the presentation	Each slide has the same design theme applied to it.
8 Switch to Slide Sorter view	In the status bar, click the Slide Sorter button.
9 Select the first slide	(If necessary.) You'll apply a different design template to the first slide.
10 Activate the Design tab	
In the Themes group, point to a theme	Point to any theme in the group, but don't display the gallery.
Right-click any theme	To display a shortcut menu.
Choose **Apply to Selected Slides**	To apply this theme to only the title slide.
11 Observe the slide	The title slide has a theme that is different from the other slides in the presentation.
12 Press (CTRL) + (Z)	To undo the theme change.
Switch to Normal view	
13 Update the presentation	

Topic B: Slide masters

This topic covers the following Microsoft Certified Application Specialist exam objectives for PowerPoint 2007.

#	Objective
1.2.1	Apply themes to slide masters
1.2.2	Format slide master backgrounds
	• Add background graphics to slide masters
	• Apply Quick Styles to backgrounds
	• Change font theme
1.3	Add elements to slide masters
	• Add slide numbers
	• Add footers
	• Add headers
	• Add placeholders
	• Add graphic elements
	• Add date and time
	• Set date and time to update automatically
4.4.1	Customize handout masters
	• Apply Quick Styles to handout masters

Slide master formatting

Explanation

All PowerPoint presentations have a slide master that controls text characteristics, background color, and certain special effects, such as shadowing and bullet styles. If you change the formatting in the slide master, the formatting for the entire presentation will be affected.

Elements of a slide master

To access the Slide Master, activate the View tab and click Slide Master.

In Slide Master view, there are two panes, as shown in Exhibit 7-3. In the left pane, the first slide is selected and eleven slides are indented under it. This indicates that the first slide is the primary master slide and the indented slides are the masters for each layout type. When you make a change to the primary master it is applied to all indented slides. When you make a change directly to one of the masters for a specific layout, the change is applied to that layout only.

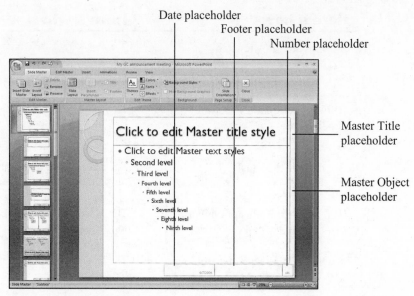

Exhibit 7-3: A slide master

On the right pane, the selected slide master is displayed, along with the various placeholders it contains. The following table describes the placeholders available on the slide master (the first slide).

Placeholder	Description
Master Title placeholder	Controls the font, size, color, style, and alignment of the slide title text.
Master Object placeholder	Controls the font, size, color, style, and alignment of the slide text, such as bulleted lists.
Number placeholder	Controls the font, size, color, style, and alignment of the slide number placeholder.
Footer placeholder	Controls the font, size, color, style, and alignment of the slide footer placeholder.
Date placeholder	Controls the font, size, color, style, and alignment of the date placeholder.

To hide or show the Number, Footer, and Date placeholders on the slide master, you can clear or check Footers in the Master Layout group. In addition, you can select any individual placeholder and press Delete to remove that placeholder. At any time, you can check Footers in the Master Layout group to again display the footer elements if they've been hidden or deleted.

Do it!

B-1:   Examining the elements of a slide master

Here's how	Here's why
1 Activate the View tab	
Click **Slide Master**	In the Presentation Views group.
2 In the left pane, select the first slide	To display the primary slide master, as shown in Exhibit 7-3. This view is also called Master view.
3 Observe the Master Title placeholder	The Master Title placeholder controls the formatting of the title placeholder on the slide.
4 Observe the Master Object placeholder	The Master Object placeholder controls the formatting of the slide text.
5 Observe the Date placeholder	The Date placeholder controls the formatting of the date and time.
6 Observe the Footer placeholder	The Footer placeholder controls the formatting of the footer. You'll enter the footer text.
7 Click the Footer placeholder	To place the insertion point.
Type **Outlander Spices**	Although you specified the footer text, by default, the footer won't appear on the presentation slides. You'll add the footer to your slides in the next activity.
8 Observe the Number placeholder	The Number placeholder controls the formatting of the slide numbers.
9 In the left pane, point to the first slide and read the ScreenTip	
	It tells you that this slide master is being used by slides 1 through 7.
10 Observe the slides in the left pane	Slide 1 is selected and there are multiple indented slides under it. The indented slides correspond to the available slide layouts.

Header and footer elements

Explanation

Even when the footer elements appear on the slide master, they still will not display on the slides in your presentation by default. To display footer elements on your presentation slides:

1   Activate the Insert tab.

2   In the Text group, click Header & Footer to open the Header and Footer dialog box, shown in Exhibit 7-4.

3   Under Include on slide, check or clear Date and time, Slide number, and Footer.

4   Click Apply to display the checked items on the current slide, or click Apply to All to apply them to all slides.

You also can use the Header and Footer dialog box to display header and footer content on notes pages and handouts pages. To do so, activate the Notes and Handouts tab, specify the content you want, and click Apply to All.

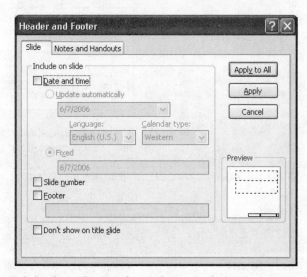

Exhibit 7-4: The Header and Footer dialog box

Do it!

B-2: Displaying header and footer elements

Here's how	Here's why
1 Activate the Insert tab	You'll indicate that you want the footer elements to appear on the slides in your presentation.
2 Click **Header & Footer**	To open the Header and Footer dialog box.
3 Check **Date & Time**	To display the date on each slide. You'll specify that the date update automatically. You'll also choose a different date format.
Verify that Update automatically is selected	
Under Update automatically, display the list and select as shown	

The specific date shown will be different, but be sure to choose the format shown.

4 Check **Slide number**	To display the slide number on each slide.
5 Check **Footer**	To activate the Footer box and place the insertion point in it. The footer text you entered on the slide master appears in the Footer box.
6 Click **Apply to All**	To apply these Header and Footer settings to all slides.
7 Click **Header & Footer**	To open the Header and Footer dialog box. You'll observe the header and footer settings for notes and handouts pages.
8 Activate the Notes and Handouts tab	No header or footer has been specified for the notes and handouts pages. You'll specify header and footer content for notes and handouts pages later in this unit.
Click **Cancel**	

Graphic elements

Explanation

Any graphic elements you add to a slide master will also appear on all slides based on that master. While viewing the slide master, activate the Insert tab and draw shapes or insert a picture or clip art just as you'd add those graphic elements to a slide.

Do it!

B-3: Adding a logo to a slide master

Here's how	Here's why
1 Verify that the Insert tab is activated	You'll insert a logo that will appear on all slides.
2 Click **Picture**	(In the Illustrations group.) To open the Insert Picture dialog box.
3 Select **Outlander Spices logo**	In the current unit folder.
Click **Insert**	The logo appears in the center of the slide master.
4 Drag the logo to the top-right corner of the slide master	
5 Activate the Slide Master tab	If necessary.
6 Click **Close Master View**	(In the Close group.) To return to Normal view.
7 View each slide	The slide logo appears on each slide, along with the footer elements. To remove the logo, you must return to Master view.
8 Return to Master view	On the View tab, click Slide Master.
9 In the left pane, select the first slide	This is the slide where you placed the logo.
10 Click the logo	To select it.
11 Press (DELETE)	To delete the logo.

Changing the font and font size on a slide master

Explanation

The slide master controls how the slides in a presentation are formatted. The slide master contains placeholders for title, text, and background items. While creating a presentation, you can emphasize the title or some of the bullet text by changing the font, size, or color in the slide master.

To change the slide format in a presentation:

1 Open the slide master, and select the Master Title placeholder.
2 Change the font, font size, or color as needed.
3 Select the Master Object placeholder.
4 Change the font, font size, or color as needed.
5 Switch to Normal view.
6 Update the presentation.

Do it!

B-4: Changing the default font

Here's how	Here's why
1 Click an edge of the Master Title placeholder	
2 Activate the Home tab	
3 From the Font list, select **Arial Narrow**	To change the title font.
Observe the Master Title placeholder	The font has changed.
4 Click an edge of the Master Object placeholder, as shown	
	To select the Master Object placeholder without placing the insertion point. If you place the insertion point, then formatting changes will apply only to the level of text containing the insertion point.
5 Change the Font to **Verdana**	To change the font for all levels.
Change the Font Size to **24**	To change the font for all levels to 24.
6 Observe the bulleted text	It looked better when each bullet level had a different font size.
Press ⌈CTRL⌋ + ⌈Z⌋	To undo the font size change.
7 Activate the Slide Master tab	
Click **Close Master View**	(Or click the Normal button in the status bar.) To exit Master view and return to Normal view.
8 Observe the presentation	The font and font size have changed for the entire presentation.
9 Update the presentation	

Modifying bullets on a slide master

Explanation

You can format the Master Object placeholder in a variety of ways. For example, you can modify the text formatting, the default bullets, the line spacing, and so on.

To modify the default bullets:

1 In Master view, select the Master Object placeholder and place the insertion point in the bullet level you want to modify.

2 Activate the Home tab.

3 In the Paragraph group, click the Bullets down arrow to display the Bullets gallery.

4 Select a bullet style.

5 Repeat steps 1 through 4 to modify other bullet levels.

6 Switch to Normal view.

Do it!

B-5: Modifying the default bullets

Here's how	Here's why
1 Go to the first slide	If necessary.
2 Switch to Master view	(Activate the View tab and click Slide Master.) You'll modify the bullets.
3 In the left pane, select the first slide	
4 In the Master Object placeholder, place the insertion point in the first line of bulleted text	You'll format the text.
5 Activate the Home tab	
In the Paragraph group, click the Bullets down arrow	To display the Bullets gallery.
Select **Star Bullets**, as shown	
6 Observe the Master Object placeholder	
	The bullet style for the first level has changed.

7   Put the insertion point in the
    second line of text

8   From the Bullets gallery, click
    Filled Square Bullets, as shown

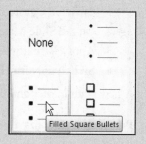

9   Return to Normal view   On the status bar, click the Normal button.

    Observe the third slide   The bullets for both the first and second levels
                                         have changed.

10 Update the presentation

Inserting slide masters

Explanation

You can have multiple slide masters in a presentation. To add a new slide master:

1 Switch to Master view.
2 On the Slide Master tab, click Insert Slide Master to insert a new slide master.
3 Apply formatting to the slide master.
4 Switch to Normal view.

A new slide master and the eleven indented slide layouts are added to the left pane.

Preserving slide masters

PowerPoint automatically deletes a slide master when it's not used by any of the slides. To prevent this, you need to preserve a slide master. By default, a new slide master is preserved when you insert it by using the Insert Slide Master button in the Edit Master group.

Slide master themes

As you view the slide master, the Slide Master tab is activated in the Ribbon by default. You can apply a different theme to the slide master by clicking Themes in the Edit Theme group and selecting a new theme. If you right-click a theme in the Themes gallery, you can use the shortcut menu to choose to apply the theme to the selected master or to create a new slide master that uses the theme.

Slide master backgrounds

If you want to apply a different background to the slide master, then on the Slide Master tab, in the Background group, click Background Styles and select a background style. In addition to the quick styles that you can select from the gallery, you can specify a custom background. To specify a custom background, click Background Styles and choose Background to open the Format Background dialog box. In the dialog box, you can specify no fill, a solid fill, a gradient fill, or a picture or texture fill. After selecting a fill type, you can specify options for that fill type and click Close to apply the background to the selected slide master. You could also click Apply to All to apply he background to all slide masters, for presentations that contain more than one slide master.

Do it!   **B-6:   Inserting a new slide master**

Here's how	**Here's why**
1 Switch to Master view	
2 In the left pane, click the first slide	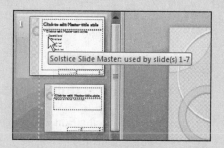
	This is the Default Design slide master, which is used by all the slides in the presentation.
3 In the Edit Master group, click **Insert Slide Master**	To insert a new slide master.
Observe the left pane and the selected slide	
	This is the new slide master you just inserted. It has a custom design and isn't being used by any slides.
4 Point as shown	
	This thumbtack icon indicates that the slide master is preserved.
In the left pane, scroll up	To observe the first slide master. Notice that the first slide master is not preserved because no icon appears next to it. Therefore, if you apply a different master to all your slides, this master will be deleted automatically.

5 Scroll down and select the second master slide	
Select the Footer placeholder	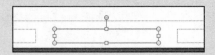
	(The center text placeholder at the bottom.) You'll enter footer text here.
Type **Outlander Spices**	
6 In the Edit Theme group, click **Themes**	To display a gallery of the available themes. The theme for the custom master you just inserted is selected.
Click the icon for the Foundry theme	You'll add this design template to the presentation. Notice that this adds another master to the presentation. If this presentation contained only one master, then the new theme would apply to that master.
7 Select the third master's first slide	
	(In the left pane.) You might need to scroll to view the third master's first slide.
Observe the left pane	There are three masters now, each with eleven indented slides. Notice that only the second master is preserved.
8 In the Edit Master group, click **Preserve**	(Or right-click the master and choose Preserve Master.) To preserve the master. The thumbtack icon appears next to the third master. This icon indicates that the master is preserved now.
9 Update the presentation	

Slide master backgrounds

Explanation

You can apply a color, gradient, pattern, or graphic to the background of a slide master to add visual interest to your slides. When you add a graphic to a slide background, you can stretch the graphic to fill all or part of each slide, or you can tile it on the slide.

To format the slide background:

1 Display Master view.
2 Select the slide master whose background you want to format.
3 In the Background group, click Background Styles and select a style or choose Format Background to open the Format Background dialog box.
4 In the Format Background dialog box, under Fill, select the fill type.
5 Specify fill settings for the fill type you selected.
6 Click Close.

Do it!

B-7: Adding slide master backgrounds

Here's how	Here's why
1 Select the second master's first slide	This master has a blank background. You'll apply a colored background.
2 Click Background Styles	(In the Background group.) To display the Background Styles gallery.
3 Select the icon for Style 6	
	Next, you'll add a graphic to the slide background.
4 Click **Background Styles** and choose **Format Background...**	To open the Format Background dialog box. The Fill settings are displayed. You can use these settings to apply a solid fill, gradient fill, or a picture or texture fill.
5 Select **Picture or texture fill**	You can insert a Texture by using the Texture list, or you can insert a picture by using the File button, Clipboard button, or Clip Art button.
6 Under Insert from, click **Clip Art**	To open the Select Picture dialog box.
In the Search text box, type **frames**	
Click **Go**	To display the relevant clip art.
7 Click as shown	
Click **OK**	To apply the clip art as a background to the second slide master
8 Drag the Transparency slider to **50%**	To apply transparency to the slide so that it appears lighter.
9 Click **Close**	

Slide master placeholders

Explanation

If you want to add an additional placeholder to a slide master, select a master layout, click Insert Placeholder in the Master Layout group, and choose the type of placeholder you want to add. You can then drag to draw the placeholder.

Do it!

B-8: Adding a placeholder to a slide master

Here's how	Here's why
1 Select the second master's Section Header layout	 You'll use this layout to create a section header slide before each new section of a presentation. You want to display a different image on each section header slide, so you'll add a picture placeholder to the slide master.
2 Click the **Insert Placeholder** down arrow	(On the Slide Master tab, in the Master Layout group.) To display the Insert Placeholder list.
3 Choose **Picture**	The pointer changes to a crosshair.
4 Drag as shown	 To create a picture placeholder centered above the text placeholders.
5 Return to Normal view	
6 Update the presentation	

Applying multiple slide masters

Explanation

After you've added multiple slide masters to a presentation, you can use these masters to add slides to the presentation. In Normal view, activate the Home tab. In the Slides group, click the New Slide down arrow to display a gallery of all the available layouts provided by the slide masters. Select a layout to apply it to a new slide. In addition, you can apply any master to existing slides. A theme for each master appears in the Themes group on the Design tab. You can select slides, right-click the theme for a master, and choose Apply to Selected Slides to apply the master to the selected slides. To apply a master to all sides, click the theme for that master.

Deleting slide masters

You can delete slide masters that are no longer necessary. When you delete a slide master, all its slide layouts are also deleted automatically.

To delete a slide master:

1 In Master view, select the slide master that you want to delete.
2 Do any of the following:

- Click the Delete button in the Edit Master group.
- Right-click to display the shortcut menu and choose Delete Master.
- Press Delete.

Do it!

B-9:   Using multiple slide masters

Here's how	Here's why
1 In the Slides group, click the **New Slide** down arrow	To display the gallery of slide layouts.
Scroll down the gallery	The first eleven are the layouts for the first master. The next eleven are the Custom Design template, and the last eleven are the Foundry master.
Under Custom Design, select **Section Header**	To add a new slide with the Section Header slide layout. This slide uses the Custom Design master. In addition, it includes the picture placeholder you added to the Section Header layout master.
2 Delete the slide	In the Slides group, click Delete.
3 Switch to Master view	
Observe the left pane	It shows three masters.
Point to each master and view the description	
4 Select the third master	You'll delete this master.
5 In the Edit Master group, click **Delete**	To delete the selected master.
6 Observe the left pane	Only two masters are left.
7 Close the Master view	
8 Update the presentation	

The handout master and notes master

Explanation

You also can view and customize the handout master and the notes master for specifying the formatting of handouts and notes pages that you can print from the presentation. To view the handout master or the notes master, activate the View tab and click the Handout Master button or the Notes Master button.

You can click Background Styles and select a quick style to apply a background color or gradient to the handout master or notes master. After you customize the handout master or notes master, click Close Master View to return to the presentation.

Do it!

B-10: Customizing the handout master

Here's how	Here's why
1 Activate the View tab	
2 Click **Handout Master**	(In the Presentation Views group.) To view the handout master. You can print one to nine slides per handout page.
3 Click **Background Styles**	(In the Background group.) To display a gallery of quick styles.
Select the background style of your choice	To apply a background style to the handout master. When you print slide handouts, they'll use the background style you specified.
4 Return to Normal view	Click Close Master View.
5 Update the presentation	

Topic C: Transitions and timings

This topic covers the following Microsoft Certified Application Specialist exam objective for PowerPoint 2007.

#	Objective
4.5.2	Rehearse and time the delivery of a presentation

Transitions

Explanation

Transitions are special effects that appear during a slide show when it moves from one slide to another. You can specify a single transition for the entire presentation, or you can specify individual transitions for each slide. You can choose from a variety of transitions and vary their speed. A good use of transition effects is to indicate a new section of a presentation or to emphasize a certain slide.

You can also set timings for your presentation so that you can run the slide show without using your mouse or keyboard to display the next slide. Instead, the slides will be displayed automatically at specified time intervals.

Transition effects for individual slides

Each slide can have a different theme and different text styles. In the same manner, you can apply different transition effects to each slide by using the Transition To This Slide group. You can set transition effects for a slide in Normal view or Slide Sorter view.

To set a transition effect for an individual slide:

1 Select the slide.

2 Activate the Animations tab. It contains the Transition To This Slide group, as shown in Exhibit 7-5.

3 In the Transition To This Slide group, point to one of the transitions to see a live preview. Click the down arrow to display the gallery of transitions and point to a transition to see the live preview. Click a transition to apply it.

Exhibit 7-5: The Transition To This Slide group

After you apply a transition to a slide, you can preview the transition by clicking the transition icon that appears on each slide.

C-1: Setting transitions for individual slides

Here's how	Here's why
1 Switch to Slide Sorter view	
Select the first slide	(If necessary.) You'll apply a transition to this slide.
2 Activate the Animations tab	
Observe the Transition To This Slide group	(As shown in Exhibit 7-5.) No transition is applied to this slide yet. On the right side of the group, you'll find the Transition Sound list, Transition Speed list, and the Apply to All button.
3 In the Transition To This Slide group, click the Dissolve transition, as shown	
	To apply it to the first slide, and see a preview of the transition.
Observe the first slide	
	Under the bottom-left corner of the slide is an icon that indicates that the slide has a transition effect applied to it.
4 From the Transition Speed list, select **Slow**	
	(In the Transition To This Slide group.) To apply the speed change and see a preview of it.
5 Run the presentation	(Click the Slide Show button in the status bar.) You'll see the transition as the first slide is displayed.
Click the mouse	(To advance to the next slide.) Notice that no transition effect has been applied.
Press (ESC)	To end the slide show.
6 Update the presentation	

Applying transition effects to the entire presentation

Explanation

To apply the same transition effect to the entire presentation:

1 View the presentation in Slide Sorter view.

2 In the Transition To This Slide group, select a transition, apply a transition sound, and change the transition speed. Or, verify the slide with the transition effect(s) is selected.

3 Click Apply To All in the Transition To This Slide group.

Applying transition effects to selected slides

Sometimes, you might want to set transition effects for only some of the slides in your presentation. You can set the transition effects for selected slides in Normal view or Slide Sorter view.

To apply transition effects to selected slides:

1 Switch to Slide Sorter or Normal view.

2 Select the slides that will have the transition effects applied to them.

3 In the Transition To This Slide group, specify the transition effects.

Do it!

C-2: Setting a transition for the entire presentation

Here's how	Here's why
1 Select the first slide	In Slide Sorter view.
2 Display the Transition gallery and click the Wipe Left transition, as shown	
	(In the Transition To This Slide group.) To apply the transition effect to the first slide.
Observe the Transition To This Slide group	The effects that are displayed for quick access have changed. They include the Wipe Left effect and those similar to it.
3 Click **Apply To All**	In the Transition To This Slide group.
4 Point as shown	
	On any slide.
Click once	To preview the transition effect.
5 Run the presentation	Click the mouse to advance slides. You'll view the transition effects for the entire presentation.
Press (ESC)	To end the slide show.
6 Select slides 2, 4, and 6	In Slide Sorter view, click slide 2; then press Ctrl and click slides 4 and 6.
Apply the Wipe Right transition effect	It is the third effect displayed on the Transition To This Slide group.
7 Run the presentation	(From the first slide.) To view the alternating transition effects.
8 Update the presentation	

Setting timings for a slide show

Explanation

You can set timings manually for each slide and then run the slide show to review the timings, or you can record timings automatically as you rehearse the presentation. Timings are useful when you want the audience to spend more time reading a specific slide. You can also use recorded timings for running a slide show in a kiosk or as a continuous background show at a convention or in a store.

To manually set the timing for a slide show using the Transition to This Slide group:

1 Clear On Mouse Click.

2 Check Automatically After.

3 Under Automatically After, set the timings between slides by entering the number of seconds in the box.

4 Click Apply to All.

Do it!

C-3:   Adding timings to a slide show

Here's how	Here's why
1 Select the first slide	In Slide Sorter view.
2 In the Transition to This Slide group, clear **On Mouse Click**	You'll set up the presentation so that it will advance to the next slide without requiring a mouse click. Instead, PowerPoint will do it automatically after a specific period of time.
Check **Automatically After**	The box under Automatically after shows 00:00.
3 Under Automatically After, click the up arrow four times	
	To set the timing to four seconds between slides.
4 Click **Apply to All**	(In the Transition To This Slide group.) To apply the transition effect to all slides in the presentation.
5 Observe the slides	
	Under each slide, you'll see the transition icon along with a timing indicator. Note that the Cover Right transition on slides 2, 4, and 6 was replaced when you clicked Apply To All. Slides
6 Run the presentation	The slides appear automatically after an interval of four seconds.
7 Update the presentation	

Rehearsing slide show timings

Explanation

You can use the Rehearse Timings feature to fine-tune your pace before you give a presentation. You can either set the timings for your slides before you rehearse, or set them automatically while you rehearse. You can use the buttons on the Rehearsal toolbar to pause between slides, restart a slide, and advance to the next slide. PowerPoint keeps track of how long each slide appears and sets the timing accordingly. When you finish your rehearsal, you can accept the timings, or you can try again.

To rehearse timings:

1   Active the Slide Show tab. In the Setup group, click Rehearse Timings to switch to Slide Show view and display the Rehearsal toolbar as shown in Exhibit 7-6.

2   Click the Next button on the Rehearsal toolbar to move through your presentation.

3   Click Yes to record the timings.

4   Press F5 to view the slide show.

Exhibit 7-6: The Rehearsal toolbar on a slide

Do it! **C-4:   Rehearsing timings**

Here's how	Here's why
1 Activate the Slide Show tab	
Observe the Set Up group	It contains the Set Up Slide Show, Hide Slide, and Rehearse Timings buttons, as well as the Record Narration button and the Use Rehearsed Timings check box.
2 Click **Rehearse Timings**	The Slide Show starts and the Rehearsal toolbar is displayed.
Observe the screen	The first slide is displayed in Slide Show view with the Rehearsal toolbar in the top-left corner. It has started recording the amount of time this slide should be displayed.
3 Press (SPACEBAR)	(Or click the Next button on the Rehearsal toolbar.) To move to the next slide. The Slide Time box returns to zero and starts counting again.
4 Every few seconds, move to the next slide	(Until the end of the presentation.) You'll see a message box.
Observe the message box	It displays the total time for the slide show.

Microsoft Office PowerPoint

The total time for the slide show was 0:00:38. Do you want to keep the new slide timings to use when you view the slide show?

[Yes]   [No]

5 Click **Yes**	To record the new slide timings, and return to Slide Sorter view.
Observe the window	The timing indicators display the new slide timings.
6 Press (F5)	To view the slide show.
View the presentation	The slides appear automatically at the specified intervals.
7 Update the presentation	

Topic D: Speaker notes

This topic covers the following Microsoft Certified Application Specialist exam objectives for PowerPoint 2007.

#	Objective
1.3	Add elements to slide masters
	• Add headers
4.4.1	Customize handout masters
	• Add headers, footers, and page numbers

Speaker notes pages

Explanation

In addition to the primary slide content, you can add speaker notes to your slides for the speaker to use as a reference. In addition, you can add headers and footers to the speaker notes pages.

Using speaker notes

Each slide can have corresponding notes to help the presenter remember key points in a presentation. Every slide in a presentation has a notes page, which contains a slide image and space for speaker notes. The presenter can use the speaker notes as a reference tool and can print them to distribute to the audience. The speaker notes don't appear onscreen during the slide show.

To add speaker notes to a slide:

1 Display the slide to which you want to add notes.
2 Activate the View tab and click Notes Page.
3 Click the notes placeholder to place the insertion point.
4 Enter the text.

You can also add speaker notes by typing in the Notes pane, which might appear below the Slides pane in Normal view. You can use the PowerPoint Options dialog box to specify whether the Notes pane appears for presentations when you open them. To do so, select the Advanced category in the PowerPoint Options dialog box, and under Display, select an option from the Open all documents using this view list. Click OK to save the new setting.

Do it!   **D-1:   Adding speaker notes**

Here's how	Here's why
1 Switch to Normal view	
Go to the first slide	If necessary.
2 Activate the View tab	
Click **Notes Page**	In the Presentation Views group.
3 Under the slide, click the notes placeholder	
	To select the text placeholder and place the insertion point in it.
4 Zoom in on the text placeholder	(Use the view controls on the status bar.) To view the text better.
5 Type the text as shown	

> Good morning! Thank you for inviting me to this month's sales meeting. I'm here to talk to you about our new product line.

| 6 Go to the last slide | (Scroll down.) You'll see a slide titled "GC Transition Team." |
| In the text placeholder, type the text, as shown | |

> Kathy Sinclair is heading up the Gourmet Collections project team for the first six months, until a new Vice President can be named. Five Outlander Spices employees and one business consultant are working with her to get the new product line to market.

| 7 Switch to Normal view | Slide 7 is selected. |
| 8 Update the presentation | |

Adding headers and footers to notes pages

Explanation

You can add headers and footers to your presentation's notes pages. A header refers to the text that appears at the top of each page in Notes Page view, and a footer refers to text that appears at the bottom of each page. You can include information such as the project name and company name in headers and footers.

To add headers and footers to notes pages:

1. On the Insert tab, click Header & Footer to open the Header and Footer dialog box.
2. Activate the Notes and Handouts tab, shown in Exhibit 7-7.
3. Under Include on page, check Header.
4. In the Header box, enter the text you want to display in the header.
5. Under Include on page, check Footer.
6. In the Footer box, enter the text you want to display in the footer.
7. Click Apply to All.

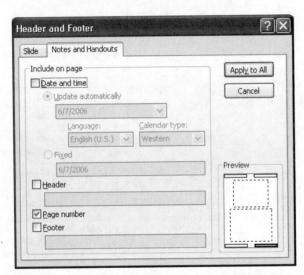

Exhibit 7-7: The Notes and Handouts tab of the Header and Footer dialog box

Do it!   **D-2:   Adding headers and footers to notes pages**

Here's how	Here's why
1 Open the Header and Footer dialog box	On the Insert tab, in the Text group, click Header & Footer.
2 Activate the Notes and Handouts tab	To display the various options on the tab, as shown in Exhibit 7-7.
3 Under Include on page, check **Date and Time**	Update automatically is selected. This means the current date will always be displayed on the slide(s).
4 Verify that Page number is checked	
5 Check **Header**	To display the header.
Under Header, enter **Gourmet Collection Rollout**	
6 Check **Footer**	To display the footer.
Under Footer, enter **Presentation for Sales Reps**	
7 Click **Apply to All**	To apply the new settings to all the notes in the presentation.
8 Display the Notes Page view	Activate the View tab and click Notes Page.
Fit the slide to the current view	(If necessary.) On the status bar, click the Fit slide to current window button.
9 Observe the notes page	You'll see the footer in the lower-left corner of the page and the header in the upper-left corner. The page number is on the bottom of the page and the date is at the top.
10 Switch to Normal view	
11 Update the presentation	

Topic E: Setting up slide shows

This topic covers the following Microsoft Certified Application Specialist exam objectives for PowerPoint 2007.

#	Objective
4.5.3	Use presentation tools
	• Use a pen and highlighter, add annotations, etc.
	• Navigate to specific slides
4.5.5	Set slide show options
	• Set presentations to loop continuously
	• Show presentation with or without narration
	• Select presentation resolution

Options for running a presentation

Explanation

PowerPoint provides multiple options for running a presentation. You can set up slide shows for different audiences and situations. The presentation might need to be run on a kiosk, at a trade show, or in a location where no one can constantly monitor the slide show. For such situations, you can use the various options in the Set Up Show dialog box.

Slide shows for speakers

When creating a presentation to accompany a speech, you can set up the presentation so that the speaker can talk while advancing slides automatically or manually. Whether the presentation advances automatically or manually, the speaker can take control of the presentation to pause it, move to any slide, or even to draw on the current slide.

During the presentation, if the presenter moves the mouse, several slide show controls appear at the bottom-left of the current slide, as shown in Exhibit 7-8. The presenter can:

- Click the arrow buttons to manually move backward or forward in the presentation.
- Click the pen icon to display a menu including pen and highlighter tools you can select for drawing on slides during a presentation. The menu also includes options for erasing ink you've drawn on the slide, for changing the ink color, and for switching back to an arrow pointer. When you end the slide show, you can choose to discard or keep your pen markings.
- Click the menu icon to display options for navigating the slide show.

Exhibit 7-8: Slide show controls

To set up a slide show for a speaker, activate the Slide Show tab. In the Set Up group, click Set Up Slide Show to display the Set Up Show dialog box, shown in Exhibit 7-9. Under Show type, select the Presented by a speaker (full screen) option and other necessary options. For example, under Show options, you can indicate whether you want the presentation to loop continuously, to be presented without any narration recorded with the presentation, and to be presented without animation effects. In addition, from the Slide show resolution list, you can specify the resolution you want to use for the slide show. A higher resolution results in a higher quality appearance of slide content. However, higher resolution values can decrease performance, causing lags in the presentation. After specifying options, click OK.

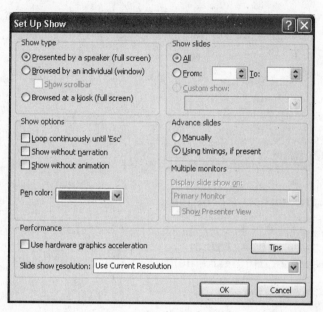

Exhibit 7-9: The Set Up Show dialog box

E-1: Setting up and running a slide show for a speaker

Here's how	Here's why
1 Display the first slide in Normal view	If necessary.
2 Activate the Slide Show tab	
In the Set Up group, click **Set Up Slide Show**	To open the Set Up Show dialog box, as shown in Exhibit 7-9.
3 Under Show type, verify that Presented by a speaker (full screen) is selected	A speaker will present this slide show.
4 Under Show slides, verify that All is selected	To show all the slides. You also can select specific slides to be shown during the slide show.
5 Under Advance slides, select **Manually**	The presenter will manually advance to the next slide.
6 Under Show options, check **Show without narration**	To specify that the slide show will run without including any recorded narration.
7 From the Slide show resolution list, select **1024x768 (Slowest, Highest Fidelity)**	(If necessary.) To specify the highest possible resolution to maximize the visual quality of the slide content during the presentation.
Click **OK**	
8 Run the slide show	
9 Move the mouse	To display the slide show controls at the bottom-left of the current slide, as shown in Exhibit 7-8.
10 Click [→]	(The navigation controls are in the bottom-left of the screen, and they are dimmed until you point to them.) To move to the next slide.
Click [←]	To return to the previous slide.
11 Click [≡]	To display the menu.
Choose **Go to Slide**, **6 Project Startup Costs**	To navigate directly to slide 6. You'll use a Pen tool to draw on this slide during the presentation.
12 Click [✎]	The pen icon.
Choose **Felt Tip Pen**	To select a felt tip pen.

13 Drag to draw a circle around the
    4th Qtr values

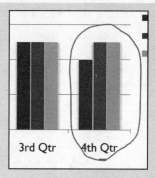

14 Click the **Pen** icon and choose   To erase the circle you drew.
    Erase All Ink on Slide

15 Click   To display the menu.

    Choose **Go to Slide**,   To navigate to slide 3.
    3 Global Product Rollout

16 Click the **Pen** icon and choose   To select the Highlighter tool.
    Highlighter

17 Drag across **$250,000 budget**

> • To be announced a
> • $250,000 budget
> Discussion

                                                To add a yellow highlight.

18 Click the **Pen** icon and choose   To return to the arrow pointer.
    Arrow

19 Press (ESC)   To return to Normal view. An alert box appears,
                                                asking you whether you want to keep your ink
                                                annotations for the next time you view the slide
                                                show.

    Click **Discard**   To remove the highlight you added.

20 Update the presentation

Slide shows for kiosks

Explanation

To customize slide shows to run on a kiosk or for a situation such as a convention, you can also use the Set Up Show dialog box. While setting up a slide show for a kiosk or booth, you need to consider several things. Will a person be there to monitor the kiosk or booth? Will you use transition effects in your presentation? Should the user be given control of the slide show?

To set up a slide show for a kiosk:

1 Open the Set Up Show dialog box.
2 Under Show type, select the Browsed at a kiosk (full screen) option.
3 Under Show slides, select the range of slides you want to include in the slide show.
4 Under Advance slides, select the options you want for controlling the pace of the presentation.
5 Click OK.

Do it!

E-2: Setting up a slide show for a kiosk

Here's how	Here's why
1 Go to the first slide	If necessary.
2 Open the Set Up Show dialog box	On the Slide Show tab, click Set Up Slide Show.
3 Under Show type, select **Browsed at a kiosk (full screen)**	Under Show options, the Loop continuously until 'Esc' option is checked and is no longer available. The slide show will loop continuously until the Esc button is pressed.
4 Under Advance slides, select **Using timings, if present**	The time settings used in the slide transition will be used to advance slides.
5 Click **OK**	To accept the changes and close the dialog box.
6 Run the presentation	After the presentation runs through once, the first slide appears again after the last slide. In addition, moving the mouse does not display the slide show controls that appeared for the speaker presentation.
Press (ESC)	To stop the slide show, or it will run continuously.
7 Update and close the presentation	

Unit summary: Modifying presentations

Topic A   In this topic, you **created a presentation based on a template**. Then, you **applied a new design theme** to quickly change the look and feel of the presentation.

Topic B   In this topic, you **examined the elements of a slide master**, changed the default font, modified the default bullets, and applied the changes to your presentation. Next, you **inserted a new slide master** and learned to **apply multiple slide masters** to your presentation.

Topic C   In this topic, you **set transitions** for individual slides and for the entire presentation. Then, you **added timings** to a slide show. Finally, you used the **Rehearse timings** feature to create a custom timing for your presentation.

Topic D   In this topic, you **added speaker notes** to individual slides. You also added **headers and footers** to notes pages.

Topic E   In this topic, you **set up a slide show for a speaker**. Then, you **set up a slide show for a kiosk**.

Independent practice activity

In this activity, you'll apply a new design theme to your presentation, change defaults in Slide Master view, insert a new slide master, and apply the new slide master to all slides. Then, you'll add transition effects, automatic timings, and speaker notes to your presentation. Next, you'll add a footer, set up the slide show for a kiosk, and run the presentation.

1 Open Progress to date.

2 Save the presentation as **My progress to date**.

3 Apply a design theme of your choice.

4 On the slide master, change the font of the Master Title placeholder to Arial Black.

5 Change the font of the Master Object placeholder to Arial Narrow.

6 Change the first-level bullet style to a style of your choice.

7 Update the presentation.

8 Add transition effects and automatic timings to all the slides.

9 Add the speaker note **Mention a few things regarding the final point** to slide 2.

10 Add the footer **Outlander Spices** to the entire presentation. (*Hint*: Use the Text group on the Insert tab.)

11 Set up the slide show for a kiosk, using automatic timings. (*Hint*: Use the Set Up group on the Slide Show tab.)

12 Run the presentation.

13 Update and close the presentation.

Review questions

1 True or false? Templates contain themes, slide masters, and title masters that provide a consistent format and look for a presentation.

2 List the steps you use to create a new presentation based on a template.

3 How can you apply a theme to an entire presentation or to selected slides?

4 How do you access the Slide Master?

5 How can you change the default format settings on the Slide Master?

6 What are transitions?

7 What happens when you apply timings to a presentation?

8 List the steps to set up a slide show to run as a kiosk.

Unit 8

Proofing and delivering presentations

Unit time: 45 minutes

Complete this unit, and you'll know how to:

A Proof a presentation for mistakes by using the Spell Check, AutoCorrect, and Thesaurus features.

B Prepare a presentation to be shown by customizing and previewing it.

C Use the Print dialog box and the Print Preview tab to specify printing options for an entire presentation, an individual slide, handouts, notes pages, and the outline.

Topic A: Proofing presentations

Explanation

After you finish creating a presentation, you need to ensure that it does not contain any mistakes. You do this by using the proofing tools, such as the Spelling and Thesaurus tools. You can also use AutoCorrect to correct common mistakes and style inconsistencies as you type.

Correcting misspelled words

When you misspell a word, it will be underlined in red by default. You can correct the spelling by using the Spelling dialog box, shown in Exhibit 8-1, or by right-clicking the misspelled word to display a shortcut menu, and choosing the correct word.

To open the Spelling dialog box, activate the Review tab, and in the Proofing group, click Spelling. You can also press F7 to open the Spelling dialog box. You can check the spelling from any view.

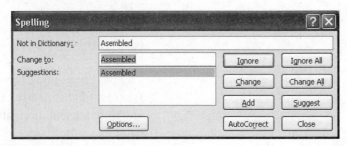

Exhibit 8-1: The Spelling dialog box

Do it!

A-1: Checking the spelling in a presentation

Here's how	Here's why
1 Open GC kickoff meeting	In the current unit folder.
2 Save the presentation as **My GC kickoff meeting**	In the current unit folder.
3 Activate the Review tab	
In the Proofing group, click **Spelling**	To open the Spelling dialog box.
4 Observe the window	You'll see the fourth slide. This is the first slide with incorrect spelling. The incorrectly spelled words are underlined in red, and the first incorrectly spelled word is highlighted in the slide.
Observe the Spelling dialog box	You'll see options to correct the spelling, as shown in Exhibit 8-1.

5 Click **Change**	(The Change button is in the Spelling dialog box.) The misspelled word "Asembled" has changed to "Assembled." Now, the text "mangement" is selected.
6 Click **Change**	To enter the correct spelling of "management." The next word, "Prelimnary" is selected.
Click **Change**	To correct the spelling to "Preliminary."
Click **Close**	To close the dialog box. You'll use a different technique to correct the next misspelled word.

7 On the fifth slide, right-click **Devloping** and choose **Developing**

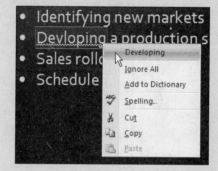

To correct the misspelled word "Devloping."

8 Press (F7)	To open the Spelling dialog box. You'll continue to check the spelling. The word "kickof" is selected.
Click **Change**	To correct the spelling of "Kickoff." A message box appears, indicating that the spelling check is complete.
Click **OK**	

9 Deselect the text

10 Update the presentation

The AutoCorrect feature

Explanation

AutoCorrect automatically corrects any typing mistakes that you make, as long as the mistakes are contained in the AutoCorrect list. You can use the AutoCorrect dialog box, shown in Exhibit 8-2, to customize AutoCorrect feature to include additional words that you misspell frequently.

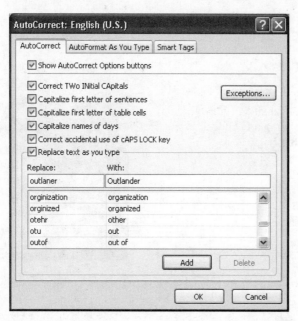

Exhibit 8-2: The AutoCorrect: English (U.S.) dialog box

Do it!   **A-2:   Using AutoCorrect**

Here's how	Here's why
1 Click the Office button	To display the menu.
At the bottom of the menu, click **PowerPoint Options**	To open the PowerPoint Options dialog box.
2 In the left pane, select **Proofing**	The Proofing options are displayed in the right pane.
Under AutoCorrect options, click **AutoCorrect Options**	To open the AutoCorrect: English (U.S.) dialog box.
3 Observe the dialog box	Notice that the insertion point appears in the Replace box. By default, all the check boxes are checked.
4 In the Replace box, enter **outlaner**	To specify a word you often mistype.
In the With box, enter **Outlander**	To specify the correct word, as shown in Exhibit 8-2.
Click **Add**	To add the word to the AutoCorrect list.
5 Click **OK**	To close the AutoCorrect: English (U.S.) dialog box.
6 Click **OK**	To close the PowerPoint Options dialog box.
7 Place the insertion point after **event**	(The last word in the fifth bullet on slide 5.) To add text here.
Press ⏎ ENTER	
8 Type **outlaner**	
Press (SPACEBAR)	The incorrect spelling is immediately corrected.
Type **Spices' new cookbook**	To complete the bullet.
9 Update the presentation	

The Thesaurus

Explanation

If you find yourself looking for just the right word to use or you want to know the general meaning of a word, you can use the Thesaurus feature. On the Review tab, in the Proofing group, click Thesaurus to open the Research pane with a list of synonyms. By reading through the list, you can get a general sense of the meaning of the word. You can also use one of the synonyms to replace the selected word.

Do it!

A-3: Using the Thesaurus

Here's how	Here's why
1 Go to the second slide	
2 Drag to select the word **inventory**	(You'll replace this word with its synonym.) Make sure you don't select the space after the word.
3 Click **Thesaurus**	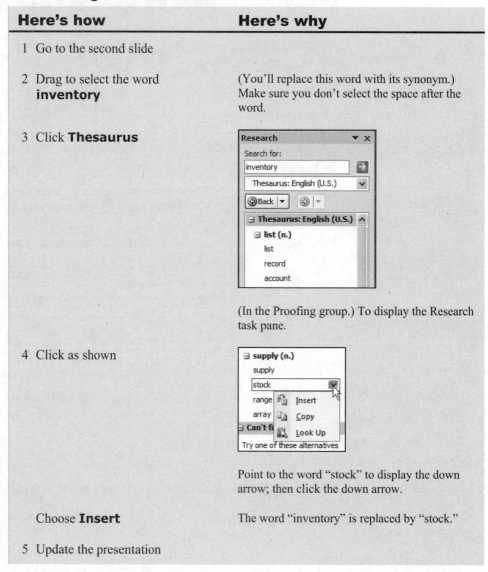 (In the Proofing group.) To display the Research task pane.
4 Click as shown	Point to the word "stock" to display the down arrow; then click the down arrow.
Choose **Insert**	The word "inventory" is replaced by "stock."
5 Update the presentation	

Topic B: Running presentations

This topic covers the following Microsoft Certified Application Specialist exam objective for PowerPoint 2007.

#	Objective
4.5.1	Show only specific slides in presentations
	• Hide specific slides

Previewing presentations

Explanation

After a presentation is complete, you are ready to show it to your audience. Before you do so, however, it's a good idea to preview it to ensure that the slide order is correct and that you want to include all the slides for this particular audience.

Previewing and running presentations

In Slide Sorter view, you can typically see the entire presentation at once to get a rough preview. There are five different techniques you can use to run the slide show, and the following table explains how each one works.

Item	Description
From Beginning button	Plays the slide show starting with the first slide, no matter what slide is selected. The From Beginning button is located in the Start Slide Show group, on the Slide Show tab.
From Current Slide button	Plays the slide show starting with the selected slide, not from the first slide. The From Current Slide button is located in the Start Slide Show group, on the Slide Show tab.
Slide Show button (Status bar)	Plays the slide show starting with the selected slide, not from the first slide. This Slide Show button is located on the status bar.
Slide Show button (View tab)	Plays the slide show starting with the first slide, no matter what slide is selected. This Slide show button is located on the View tab.
Press F5	Plays the slide show starting with the first slide, no matter what slide is selected.

Do it!

B-1: Previewing and running a presentation

Here's how	Here's why
1 Switch to Slide Sorter view	
2 Select the fourth slide	
3 Click 🖵	To switch to Slide Show view. Notice that the slide show begins from the fourth slide.
4 Move through the slides until you reach the end of the presentation	
Press (ESC)	
5 Observe the window	The presentation is in Slide Sorter view.
6 Update the presentation	

Hiding and unhiding slides

Explanation

When you create a presentation, you might want to use it for more than one audience. In that case, you might want to include some slides for one audience that are not included for another audience. You can hide individual slides so they aren't displayed in Slide Show view.

To hide a slide, select the slide and activate the Slide Show tab. In the Set Up group, click Hide Slide. The Hide Slide button works as a toggle. When you want to show a hidden slide again, you select that slide and click Hide Slide. Hidden slides remain visible in Normal view, but won't appear during a slide show.

Do it!

B-2:   Hiding and unhiding a slide

Here's how	Here's why
1 Select the last slide	You'll hide this slide.
2 Activate the Slide Show tab	
In the Set Up group, click **Hide Slide**	
3 Observe the slide	
	A box appears around the slide number, and a line appears over the slide number.
4 Select the first slide	
5 Run the presentation	
Move through the presentation	You'll see that the Outstanding issues slide does not appear in the slide show.
6 Select the fifth slide	
Click **Hide Slide**	To unhide the slide.
7 Update the presentation	

Topic C: Printing presentations

This topic covers the following Microsoft Certified Application Specialist exam objectives for PowerPoint 2007.

#	Objective
1.4.1	Change presentation orientation
1.4.3	Set slide size
4.4.2	Print a presentation in various formats
	• Slides
	• Handouts
	• Outlines
	• Notes

Presentation previews

Explanation

By default, PowerPoint creates presentations in color. If you want to print the presentation in black and white, you might want to preview it to ensure that the colors have appropriate contrast when converted to black and white.

Previewing presentations in black and white

To preview a presentation in black and white, activate the View tab and click Pure Black and White. To preview a presentation in gray, click Grayscale.

Do it!

C-1: Previewing a presentation in black and white

Here's how	Here's why
1 Switch to Normal view	
Activate the View tab	
2 Click **Pure Black and White**	(In the Color/Grayscale group.) To preview how the slides will appear in black and white.
3 Observe the slides	All the colors have changed to black and white.
4 Click **Back To Color View**	(On the Black And White tab, in the Close group.) To display the slides in color.
5 Update the presentation	

Modifying page setup

Explanation

You can print slides in a variety of formats, but the presentation's page setup determines the size and orientation of the printed output. In PowerPoint, size refers to the size of the slide on a printed page, and orientation refers to whether the pages are set up as portrait (tall) or landscape (wide). The default settings for any new presentation are for an on-screen slide show with landscape orientation. The slide numbering begins with 1. Handouts, outlines, and notes print in portrait orientation by default. You can change these settings.

To change the page setup for slides:

1　Activate the Design tab.

2　In the Page Setup group, click Page Setup to open the Page Setup dialog box.

3　From the Slides sized for list, select the format of your choice.

4　Under Orientation, select an orientation (Portrait or Landscape) for the slides and the other components of the presentation.

5　Click OK.

You also can change the orientation by clicking Slide Orientation in the Page Setup group, and choosing Portrait or Landscape.

Slide size format options

The following table describes some of the size format options in the Page Setup dialog box.

Format	Description
On-screen Show	This is the default setting. Use it when designing a presentation you plan to show on screen. The slides are sized smaller than a standard sheet of paper.
Letter Paper (8.5×11 in)	Prints the presentation on standard U.S. letter stock (8.5" × 11").
Ledger Paper (11×17 in)	Prints the presentation on standard U.S. ledger stock (11" × 17").
A3 Paper (297×420 mm)	Prints the presentation on an international letter stock (297 mm × 420 mm).
A4 Paper (210×297 mm)	Prints the presentation on an international letter stock (210 mm × 297 mm).
35mm Slides	This setting, which is smaller than the default setting, adapts the presentation to 35mm slides.
Overhead	Prints your slides on overhead transparency stock (8.5" × 11").
Banner	Adjusts the slide size to create an 8" × 1" banner when printed.
Custom	Use this setting to adjust the slide size to accommodate special sizing needs.

Do it!

C-2:   Modifying the page setup

Here's how	Here's why
1 Activate the Design tab	
2 In the Page Setup group, click **Slide Orientation**	To display the menu.
Choose **Portrait**	To change the page orientation.
3 Click **Slide Orientation** and choose **Landscape**	To return the page orientation to its default setting.
4 In the Page Setup group, click **Page Setup**	To open the Page Setup dialog box.
5 From the Slides sized for list, select **A4 Paper (210x297mm)**	
6 Under Slides, select **Portrait**	Notice that the width and height boxes change automatically.
7 Verify that the Number slides from box reads **1**	To apply the page setup from slide 1 onwards.
8 Click **OK**	(To close the Page Setup dialog box.) The change in page setup is reflected in the slide on the screen.
9 Press (CTRL) + (Z)	To undo the last step and restore the default page setup.

Printing presentations

Explanation

When you click the Office button and choose Print, the Print dialog box opens, as shown in Exhibit 8-3. In this dialog box, you can specify the printer that you'll use, the range of slides you'll print, the number of copies, and so on.

Printing overhead transparencies

If you're using a black-and-white printer to create overhead transparencies, you should preview the slides in black and white before printing. You can then make any necessary adjustments before printing your presentation directly on overhead transparency stock.

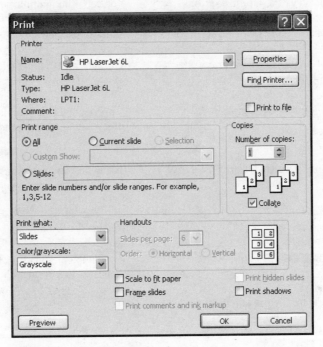

Exhibit 8-3: The Print dialog box

Do it!

C-3: Printing a presentation

Here's how	Here's why
1 Click the Office button and choose **Print**	To open the Print dialog box, as shown in Exhibit 8-3.
2 Observe the Print range options	If you have a multiple-slide presentation, you can print a specific range. By default, All is selected.
3 Observe the Copies options	You can print multiple copies, collated or not.
4 Observe the Print what options	Slides is selected.
5 Observe the Color/grayscale options	You can print in grayscale, pure black and white, or color.
6 Click **Preview**	A preview of how your presentation will look after printing appears, and the Print dialog box closes.
Click **Close Print Preview**	(In the Preview group on the Print Preview tab.) To close the Preview window and return to Normal view.
7 Press (CTRL) + (P)	To open the Print dialog box.
Click **OK**	To print the presentation. If your computer isn't connected to a printer, click Cancel.
8 Update the presentation	

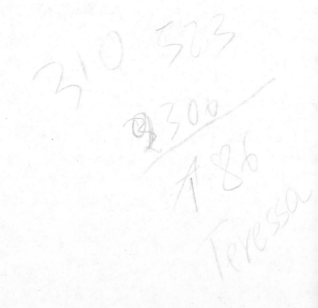

Printing individual slides

Explanation

You can also print an individual slide from a presentation. To do so:

1 Select the slide you want to print.

2 Click the Office button and choose Print (or press Ctrl+P) to open the Print dialog box.

3 Under Print range, select Current slide.

4 Click OK.

In the Print dialog box, you can also specify the number of copies of that slide that you want to print.

Do it!

C-4: Printing an individual slide

Here's how	Here's why
1 Select the first slide	If necessary.
2 Open the Print dialog box	Press Ctrl+P.
3 Under Print range, select **Current slide**	You'll print only the first slide.
4 Click **Preview**	To open the Preview. On the left side of the status bar, notice that it reads "Page 1 of 1" indicating that only one page will be printed.
Click **Close Print Preview**	To close the Preview.
5 Update the presentation	

Print output options

PowerPoint provides multiple print output options. You can print slides, handouts, speaker notes, or a presentation outline. You use the Print what list in the Print dialog box to specify the type of output you want to create. In addition, when you preview the items you plan to print, you can use the options on the Print Preview tab to specify many of the same options available in the Print dialog box.

Audience handouts

You can specify options for printing audience handouts for your presentation by using the Print dialog box or the Print Preview tab. You can print these handouts with one, two, three, four, six, or nine slides per page. When you're deciding how many slides to include per page, consider the readability of the handout. If you include too many slides with text, the handouts might be difficult for your audience to read.

To print audience handouts:

1   Click the Office button and choose Print.
2   From the Print what list, select Handouts.
3   Under Handouts, from the Slides per page list, select the number of slides you want to include on each page.
4   Click OK.

In addition, on the Print Preview tab, you can specify the number of handouts to print by selecting from the Print What list. You can use the Print What list to specify that you want to preview (and print) slides, handouts, notes pages, or an outline.

Speaker notes

You can print speaker notes for your presentation as well. Each page of speaker notes includes a small version of the associated slide. This will help you keep track of your progress as you deliver your presentation.

To print speaker notes:

1   Click the Office Button and choose Print.
2   From the Print what list, select Notes Pages.
3   Under Print range, select Slides.
4   In the Slides box, enter the slide range of your choice. For example, you can print the speaker notes for slides 1, 2, 3, 4, and 7 by entering "1–4, 7".
5   Click OK.

Outlines

If you want to print the text from your presentation slides, then you can print Outline view. When you print Outline view, you print the text shown in the Outline tab. To do so, in the Print dialog box, from the Print what list, select Outline View, and click OK.

C-5:   Printing handouts, notes, and the outline

Here's how	Here's why
1 Open the Print dialog box	
2 Under Print range, select **All**	

3   From the Print what list, select **Handouts**

To specify that you want to print audience handouts of the presentation slides.

    Observe the Handouts options

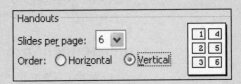

You can specify how many slides you want to print on a single page. In addition, you can specify how the slides are ordered on the handout.

4   Under Handouts, select **Vertical**

Notice the vertical ordering of the slides in the preview on the right.

5   Open the Preview

(Click Preview.) To preview the slide handouts. You'll preview other settings by choosing options on the Print Preview tab.

You'll preview the notes pages.

6   Display the Print What list and observe

(In the Page Setup group.) You can quickly switch to what you want to print by selecting Slides, Notes Pages, Outline View, or one of the Handout options.

    Select **Notes Pages**

To change what you are going to print from handouts to notes pages.

7   Click **Options**

To display the Options menu. You can access the Header and Footer dialog box, change the Color/Grayscale options, modify the Printing Order, and so on.

    Close the Options menu

8   Click **Print**

(In the Print group.) To return to the Print dialog box.

9   From the Print what list, select **Outline View**

10   Preview the Outline view

Click Preview.

11   Click **Close Print Preview**

(In the Preview group on the Ribbon.) To return to Normal view without printing.

12   Update and close the presentation

Unit summary: Proofing and delivering presentations

Topic A   In this topic, you **corrected spelling mistakes** by using the Spell Check feature. Then, you customized the **AutoCorrect** feature. Finally, you used the **Thesaurus** to replace a word with a synonym.

Topic B   In this topic, you previewed **and ran the presentation in Slide Show view**. Next, you **hid slides** and **unhid slides**.

Topic C   In this topic, you **previewed a presentation in black and white**. You also **modified the page setup**. Finally, you learned how to **print** an entire presentation, individual slides, handouts, notes, and the outline.

Independent practice activity

In this activity, you'll check a presentation for spelling mistakes, run the presentation in Slide Show view, and print the slides.

1 Open Products.

2 Save the presentation as **My products**.

3 Check the spelling of the entire presentation. (*Hint*: Use options on the Review tab.)

4 Run the presentation (starting from the first slide).

5 Print the presentation (if your computer is connected to a printer). If you don't have access to the printer, view the slides in Print Preview.

6 Print the presentation as a handout with 2 slides per page (if your computer is connected to a printer). If you don't have access to the printer, view the handouts in Print Preview.

7 Update and close the presentation.

8 Close PowerPoint.

Review questions

1 True or false? When you misspell a word, it will be underlined in green by default.

2 Select the correct methods for correcting a spelling mistake. (Choose all that apply.)

A Use the Spelling dialog box.

B Right-click anywhere on the slide and choose the correct word.

C Use the Spelling and Grammar dialog box.

D Right-click the misspelled word and choose the correct word.

3 What does the AutoCorrect feature do?

4 How do you access the Thesaurus feature?

5 True or false? When you click the Slide Show button in the status bar, the slide show always starts at the first slide.

6 True or false? When you click the Slide Show button on the View tab, the slide show always starts at the selected slide, not the first slide.

7 True or false? When you press F5 the slide show starts at the selected slide, not the first slide.

8 List the steps you perform to hide a slide.

9 List the steps you perform to print audience handouts.

Course summary

This summary contains information to help you bring the course to a successful conclusion. Using this information, you will be able to:

A Use the summary text to reinforce what you've learned in class.

B Determine the next courses in this series (if any), as well as any other resources that might help you continue to learn about PowerPoint 2007.

Topic A: Course summary

Use the following summary text to reinforce what you've learned in class.

Unit summaries

Unit 1

In this unit, you opened a presentation and viewed it as a **slide show**. Then, you examined the **PowerPoint environment**, and switched among Normal, Slide Sorter, and Slide Show views. Next, you adjusted **magnification** in Normal view and used **PowerPoint Help**.

Unit 2

In this unit, you **created a new presentation, added slides, entered text**, and **edited the text**. You used the Save As dialog box **to save a presentation**, and **updated a presentation** by using the Save command. Then, you used the Save As dialog box to **save a presentation in a new location**. You **moved slides** in both Normal view and Slide Sorter view. Next, you **deleted slides**. Finally, you **inserted slides from another presentation** into your presentation.

Unit 3

In this unit, you applied **character formatting** to selected text by using commands in the Font group and Mini toolbar. Next, you used the **Format Painter** to repeat text formatting. Then, you changed **bulleted styles** and applied a **numbered list**. You used the **Find** dialog box to search for specific text, and the **Replace** dialog box to replace text. Next, you used the **Cut, Copy**, and **Paste** commands to move text to another slide. You used the **Clipboard pane** to copy and paste multiple items. Finally, you applied **paragraph formatting**.

Unit 4

In this unit, you used drawing tools to **create basic shapes**, and **applied formatting to selected objects**. Next, you **duplicated, deleted**, and **moved objects**. Then, you **modified objects** by resizing and rotating them. You **aligned multiple objects** to one another. And finally, you **added text to an object, modified text in an object**, and **drew a text box** on a slide.

Unit 5

In this unit, you **added a WordArt object** to a slide. Then, you **modified a WordArt object** by applying different styles. Next, you **inserted an image** file. You **modified the picture** and **grouped images** together. Then, you **inserted a clip art image**, and **modified the clip art** image. And finally, you inserted a clip art image from the **Web Collections**.

Unit 6

In this unit, you **added a table** to a slide, and **modified** and **formatted the table**. You also **created a chart**, and **modified the chart** by changing its formatting. Next, you **added a SmartArt hierarchy chart** to a slide, and **modified the hierarchy chart** by formatting it and adding additional boxes.

Unit 7

In this unit, you **created a presentation based on a template**. Then, you **applied a new design theme** to quickly change the look and feel of the presentation. Next, you **examined the elements of a slide master**, changed the default font, modified the default bullets, and applied the changes to your presentation. You **inserted a new slide master** and **applied multiple slide masters** to a presentation. Then, you **set transitions** for individual slides and for the entire presentation. Next, you **added timings** to a slide show. You used the **Rehearse timings** feature to create a custom timing for your presentation, **added speaker notes** to individual slides, and **added footers** to each slide in your presentation. Next, you added headers and footers to notes pages. Finally, you **set up a slide show for a speaker**, and **set up a slide show for a kiosk**.

Unit 8

In this unit, you **corrected spelling mistakes** by using the Spell Check feature, customized the **AutoCorrect** feature, and used the **Thesaurus** to replace a word with a synonym. Then, you previewed **and ran the presentation in Slide Show view**, **hid** and **unhid slides**, and **previewed a presentation in black and white**. You also **modified the page setup**. Finally, you learned how to **print** an entire presentation, individual slides, handouts, and notes.

Topic B: Continued learning after class

It is impossible to learn to use any software effectively in a single day. To get the most out of this class, you should begin working with PowerPoint 2007 to perform real tasks as soon as possible. Course Technology also offers resources for continued learning.

Next course in this series

This is the first course in this series. The next course in this series is:

- *PowerPoint 2007: Advanced*
    - Customize the PowerPoint environment
    - Customize design themes and templates
    - Insert sounds, movies, and animations
    - Customize clip art, IGX graphics, and tables
    - Create custom slide shows
    - Share presentations in various formats
    - Review presentations
    - Integrate Microsoft Office files

Other resources

For more information, visit www.course.com.

PowerPoint 2007: Basic

Quick reference

Button	Shortcut keys	Function
		Displays a list of commonly used file commands.
	PAGE UP	Moves to the previous slide.
	PAGE DOWN	Moves to the next slide.
		Switches to Normal view.
		Switches to Slide Sorter view.
	F5	Runs the slide show.
	ESC	Ends a slide show.
		The Fit slide button returns the slide view to the default percentage.
	CTRL + W	Closes a presentation.
	ALT + F4	Closes the PowerPoint application.
	F1	Opens Microsoft Office Word Help.
	CTRL + Z	Undoes the last action.
	CTRL + Y	Redoes the last action that was undone.
	CTRL + S	Saves the current presentation.
	CTRL + A	Selects all the text within the placeholder.
B	CTRL + B	Applies bold formatting to the selected text.
I	CTRL + I	Applies italic formatting to the selected text.
U	CTRL + U	Applies underline formatting to the selected text.

Button	Shortcut keys	Function
S		Applies shadow formatting to the selected text.
		Activates the tool to copy the formatting of the selected text to other text. Double-click to lock the Format Painter so you can format text multiple times.
	CTRL + X	Cuts the selected text or object.
	CTRL + C	Copies the selected text or object.
	CTRL + V	Pastes the first text or object from the Clipboard.
	CTRL + L	Aligns the selected paragraph to the left.
	CTRL + E	Centers the selected paragraph.
	CTRL + R	Aligns the selected paragraph to the right.
	CTRL + J	Justifies the selected paragraph.
		Activates the tool, located on the Insert tab in the Shape group, to draw a rectangle on the slide.
	CTRL + D	Duplicates a selected object.
		Activates the tool, located in the Shape group, to draw a text box on the slide.
A		Changes text fill color, removes the fill, or adds a gradient or a texture.
		Changes text, outlines color, and provides other options.
		Changes specific effects, such as Shadow, Reflection, Glow, Bevel, 3-D Rotation, and Transform.
		Centers text between the top and bottom edges of the text placeholder.
		Adds bulleted list formatting.
		Adds numbered list formatting.
		Displays text in two or more columns.

Shortcut keys	Function
CTRL + P	Opens the Print dialog box.
F7	Check the spelling in a presentation.
CTRL + F	Opens the Find and Replace dialog box.
SHIFT + TAB	In a table, moves one cell to the left.
ALT + HOME	In a table, moves to the first cell in a row.
ALT + END	In a table, moves to the last cell in a row.
ALT + PAGE UP	In a table, moves to the first cell in the column.
ALT + PAGE DOWN	In a table, moves to the last cell in the column.

Glossary

Align left

When applied, the lines of text are aligned along the left side of the text placeholder, and the right side of the paragraph appears ragged.

Align right

When applied, the lines of text are aligned along the right side of the text placeholder, and the left side looks ragged.

AutoCorrect

Automatically corrects any typing mistakes that you make, as long as the mistakes are contained in the AutoCorrect list.

Cell

The smallest part of a table. It is defined by the intersection of a row and a column.

Character formatting

Any formatting that you can apply to individual characters, and includes changing the font, font size, and type style (bold, italic, and underlining).

Charts

A graphical representations of numeric data. PowerPoint includes several chart types for you to choose from and includes multiple formatting options that you can use to modify them.

Clipboard

A temporary storage area that holds the text or object you have copied or pasted until you specify where to place it in a document. The Clipboard can hold only one selection at a time and is cleared when you shut down your computer.

Copy

The Copy command creates a copy of the selected text or object on the Clipboard.

Cut

The Cut command removes the selected text or object to the Clipboard.

Grid

A set of intersecting lines that appear on a slide.

Guide

A pair of horizontal and vertical nonprinting lines that intersect the in middle of the slide but can also be moved.

Justify

When applied, the lines of text are evenly distributed to the left and right sides of the placeholder. Neither the left nor right side of the paragraph appears ragged.

Live preview

When you move the pointer over options in a gallery or list that uses live preview, each option is previewed on the current slide. For example, moving the pointer over each font in the Font list causes any selected text on the current slide to appear in that font temporarily.

Office button

Click to display a menu of options. In previous versions of PowerPoint, it was the File menu.

Mini toolbar

A floating palette that appears immediately after you select text on a slide. The Mini toolbar contains some of the formatting options available in the Font and Paragraph groups. After you select some text, the Mini toolbar appears, but is almost transparent until you activate it by pointing to it.

Normal view

The default view, which you'll usually work in as you create slides. It contains two tabs on the left and a Slide pane on the right. The two tabs on the left are the Slides tab and the Outline tab.

Paragraph formatting

Any formatting that can apply only to whole paragraphs, and includes text alignment, line spacing, bulleted list, numbered list, and so on.

Paste

The Paste command takes the text or object from the Clipboard and inserts a copy of it wherever the insertion point is positioned.

Quick Access toolbar

Contains frequently used commands (by default, Save, Undo, Repeat/Redo, and Print). Can be customized to include the commands you specify.

Ribbon

Contains PowerPoint's primary tools, commands, and other features, divided among tabs named Home, Insert, Design, Animations, Slide Show, Review, View, and Developer, as well as several contextual tabs. The items in each tab are organized into several groups.

Ribbon groups

Named groupings of controls within a tab. Each tab contains several groups.

Scrollbars

You can use the horizontal and vertical scrollbars to view parts of the presentation that don't currently fit in the window.

Slide

Displays the text and graphics that you type and edit.

Slide Show view

Provides a full-screen view of your presentation. Any special effects you add to your presentation, such as transitions and timings, are visible during the slide show.

Slide Sorter view

Provides a miniature view of all the slides in a presentation so you can view multiple slides at once. You can arrange the order of the slides by using this view.

Status bar

Contains the status information, View button, window switching buttons, and the document zoom slider.

Title bar

Displays the name of the current document.

Transitions

Are special effects that appear during a slide show when it moves from one slide to another. You can specify a single transition for the entire presentation, or you can specify individual transitions for each slide.

WordArt

A text object that has pre-designed effects that are applied when you create the object.

Index